The Dirty Secrets to Buying a Business Everyone is Afraid to Tell You

You Don't Need Experience or to Risk Your Own Money to Buy Your First or Next Business...

Arturo Henriquez

ISBN-13: 978-0692151976 (Arturo Henriquez)

ISBN-10: 0692151974

This book is dedicated to my Family!

I am forever grateful to my mother and father who opened the doors of opportunity and taught me the most valuable lesson of all; To have a deep sense of personal responsibility. I am grateful to my loving wife and my two lovely daughters who constantly inspire me to be a better man. And I am grateful to my brothers and sister for their unconditional love and support.

I am who I am because of all of you!

Table of Contents

Introduction

In this book you will learn why anybody can buy a small business with little or no experience and in most cases without using any of their money or, better yet, using somebody else's money. While this sounds like it is easier said than done, you'd be surprised how many times there are multiple million dollar businesses that are purchased without using one's own capital and by people that do not have experience in the same industry. This a day in day out reality. There is vast availability of debt and equity in the market from either institutions or private lenders or financiers or equity holders or the owners themselves. The deals we have structured have an outsider financier component for the majority of the purchase price. And we have done many successful deals without our cash or equity at stake. We'll get into that in the upcoming chapters. But, essentially, anybody is really one deal away from buying a business and completely transforming their life.

Most people think buying a business is an insurmountable event. It is something that is beyond their reach. How do you run a business? How do you understand the financials? Where do I get the money to buy this business? How do I deal with employees? How do I deal with suppliers? Can I really do this? I don't know anything about the product or the service? I don't know anything about the industry? Where do I start? These and thousands of other questions usually prevent most people from going out and buying a business. The irony is that buying a business is not that difficult. And I would venture to say it is easy when properly guided. All these doubts and concerns are in people's minds and prevent them from trying, from venturing. It really is not that hard. I have done this for over 25 years. And the truth is, whether you buy a restaurant, a distribution company, a technology company, a dry cleaner, a gym, or pretty much any small business, there are common denominators in every business that I purchased that can be easily learned by anybody. Business fundamentals and learning how to buy a business all share the same guidelines. Followed correctly, anyone can buy a business. You are really only ONE deal away from completely transforming your life.

Buying a business is a life altering event. You are no longer bound to a corporate job. You are your own boss. You are able to guide your own life. You obtain financial freedom, professional independence, stature and more importantly, you begin to create wealth. Done properly, buying a business is very easy to do. It is no different than buying a home. And most people buy one home in their lifetime, if not multiple homes. Obviously, there needs to be tenacity and hard work is required. There is detail and there is knowledge to be learned. There is experience to be obtained. But I have set up the sequence of this book into a step by step process where I put 25 years of experience in deal making, whether for myself or for others, all down into a very easy, step by step guide to buying a business. This is what the book is all about. You will learn a methodology and psychology to make that deal materialize into your reality. I will teach you how to buy a business and you will see that all those things that have always prevented you from buying a business begin to dissipate, to fade away. All those doubts, all those unknowns, all those mysteries, all those cants' will all disappear. Buying a business is a game changer. And anyone can do it.

So let me talk a little bit about myself and my over 25-year journey in deal making. I have been an entrepreneur for over 25 years. I'm 47 years old as of the writing this book and have been involved in well over 130 business purchases and business deals.

I have successfully started, bought and or sold over 45 companies personally for my own portfolio. In some cases, I have had partners, mostly operating partners. I have bought many restaurants, started a tequila company, a consumer goods export company, a technology company, I have bought bars and night clubs, a pest control company, fast food restaurants, real estate brokerages, a steel fabrication company, franchises, wholesale distributers, a NAP, a loan servicing company, a logistics company, an import and distributor of electrical appliances, an oil and gas company, a theatre production, a professional soccer game, a senior living management company, among others. These have all been done by me for my own portfolio.

I have raised money from friends and families. I have raised money from venture capital funds like Merrill Lynch Venture Capital, CVC Latin America which is Citibank's venture capital arm as well as Explorador fund in Silicon Valley. I've taken a company public on the stock market in the United States, what is commonly known as an IPO or initial public offering. And I have done corporate takeovers as an entrepreneur. And I have raised millions of dollars from banks, asset based lending institutions and angel investors. All of this for my portfolio companies previously mentioned.

In addition to the businesses I have bought and sold, I have been involved in over 30 deals or transactions where I risked my own capital. These are somewhat different than buying a business, yet obey in most part the general guidelines of buying a business.

I have worked in Wall Street and other mergers and acquisitions and financial institutions over the past 25 years where I participated in over 60 transactions that were directly involved in the buying and selling of businesses. I've worked for the likes of Bank of America, Goldman Sachs, Lehman Brothers, this is the Lehman Brothers long before it dissolved and went into bankruptcy in fact over 10 years before that, back in 1999 when Lehman Brothers was the lean mean fighting machine on Wall Street. I've worked as managing director at KPMG where I spearheaded their mergers and acquisition department from start up to multiple deals a year in pipeline. In the corporate world I have sold companies (divestitures). I've bought business. I've helped companies raise funds via private equity. I have restructured companies. I have divested parts of companies. I was involved in valuations, financial advisories, due diligences, and financial and operational restructurings.

I also want to point out that I have invested in my education and I cannot stress enough how important this is. Investment in one's education is probably the single best investment that my family made in me and that I then made in myself and I continue to make in myself to this day. There is no substitute for learning best practices. I have three Master's degrees (Post-graduate), a Master's in Business Administration (MBA) Kellogg Graduate School of Management at Northwestern University and a double Master's in International Relations and Communications from Boston University. There is no substitute for learning how to do things differently. There is no substitute for creativity. Having practical, hands on experience in real life I believe needs to be balanced with theory. Just plain life experience I believe is not enough. If you're out there hustling, you're out there deal making and you're so involved in your own everyday businesses, it's hard to take a step back and gain perspective. It is hard to take a step back and see what else you're missing. Questions like what else can I apply to this business? What else can I apply to my Deal making Strategies? What am I missing? What are the new funding source? What are the new technologies that are out there? What does the new marketing and advertising look like? What are the best practices today? Where is this industry heading in 5, 10 even 20 years and what is driving these changes? Ten years ago online advertising wasn't even on the horizon. Today, it's hard to survive without having an online presence let alone proactive online marketing and advertising strategies. And this is no longer new, yet I know most small businesses are not employing this because that have not taken the time to learn and reeducate themselves about their business and everything that affects it. By education, I don’t mean go out and get a graduate degree. I mean always have one foot in education, in theory, in academia. There are online courses. There are many local educational programs. And yes, to those that see the value, there are undergraduate and graduate programs and diplomas. You will be more enriched and you will have that ever so important balance between theory and real life experiences. Having both makes for a lethal preparation for really anything that you do not just professional but personal. Trust Me.

So all in all at the age of 47, as an entrepreneur, financier, private equity and professional, have been involved in well over 130 businesses and business deals. And I have done deals of all shapes, sizes and colors. So a very long curriculum in my background with regards to buying businesses. So needless to say I've been around the block a couple of time and seen pretty much everything. To use a famous quote, "I know a thing or two about a thing or two" when it comes to buying businesses, deal making and anything surrounding it.

The whole point of this book is to teach you a simple, proven step by step process to buy business. And I want to make it crystal clear that anybody from all walks of lives, whether you're 20 years old or 70 years old or any age in between, whether you have experience in a certain sector or you don't, whether you have bought businesses and been successful or failed at them, whether you're in the corporate world, whether you have or don't have financial resources, whether you have a home based business, whether you're a waiter at a restaurant or working in a factory or a restaurant or what not. This can be done by anyone without experience. If you follow the step by step process, I am certain you can buy a business. You can buy it without risking your own capital. It's easier said than done. There's a whole method to the madness. A lot of pieces have to come into play. But when they do you can leverage the assets of the company, you could have what's called owner financing, which is when the owner actually finances the transaction, most of my deals are like this. All of the businesses that I have bought all have a big or small element of owner financing. And then other forms of financing and funding from either investors or financial institutions. A very effective way is to leverage the existing assets of the business, the target company, to buy the business. This is commonly referred to as a Leverage Buy Our or an LBO. And so more likely than not you can come across businesses where you can not only buy them where you have no experience but where you can buy them without risking your own capital.

Follow each chapter because this book is sequential. It starts off with the small business space and the many reasons not to start a new business or start a new franchise. We explore you and why you want to buy a business, what is your objective, your end game. Then the type of business you want in terms of location, size, industry, resources among other thigs. We explore the various types of sellers and we dive deep into the psychology of the prototypical seller we will source more than 80% of our deals from. We explore the many different sourcing strategies and go into detail as to all the various ways to find businesses and motivated sellers. We explain about the actual meeting strategies once you have identified a business and a motivated Seller, how to approach them and how to position yourself. We talk about different valuation methods to value a business, methodologies used by investment banks and the big accounting firms, KPMG, Earns & Young, Price Waterhouse and Deloitte. And the most commonly used valuation method used for valuing small business. We then talk about structuring a deal and getting to an LOI, a letter of intent, which is essentially your offer. Once you have an offer in place we go about structuring the financial side and how we raise the necessary capital and from what sources. Then we move forward with the due diligence to validate the business in all its forms, to the legal documentation all the way to the closing, with some final tips as to what to do after. So I recommend you read it first from start to finish in sequential order to get the bigger picture. You can always return to the various chapters to look over specific topics afterwards.

In this book you will understand from point A to point Z, all the ins and outs of buying a business. And from a practical perspective, not theory. You will understand that most things, most steps are very logical and rely on a high degree of common sense. There's a lot of hard work on your end that you need to do. But it is not complicated and very doable. And anyone can do it. Trust me, I have done it multiple times. But you do need guidance and a step by step proven system that has worked for others and particularly has worked for me. I know my system is being used by many other people. This needs to be coupled with hard work, perseverance and the confidence in yourself to get it done. You will not be successful at anything without this. I know you know this but it needs to be said. You will not be successful if you don't put the hard work that success requires of anyone. Nobody gets success handed to them. You have to have perseverance. And lastly you have to have confidence in yourself. The biggest reason why people aren't buying businesses is because of their mindset. They are the obstacle. It's their fear, self-doubt and their lack of confidence that prevents them from taking action. Can I do this? Do I have the skill set to do this? Is this for me? Things like, are they for people like me? What happens if I do this and I actually buy a business? Will I be able to run it? Will I be able to operate it? Am I getting myself into deep? All of this really comes down to self-doubt, a symptom of fear. People are scared and hence will not take action. And so you have to have confidence in your ability to do this. This can be done. I will become your mentor through this book. This book is a Step by Step proven system. I am giving you that with this book. But the self-confidence, that has to come from deep within. And that's absolutely vital for this and for whatever else you do in life.

I'm putting over 25 years of experience, successes, failures, lessons learned, tough moments, exhilarating moments all in this book. So what was a 25 year learning curve for me to get to a point of success and financial freedom and professional independence, is now condensed into a short and very direct practical and implementable plan of action for you to achieve your objective of becoming a business owner and buying a business in months and not the 25 years that it took me. Just remember, you are one deal away from a seven-digit company. You are one deal away from financial freedom. You are one deal away from independence. Your one deal away from being your own boss. You are one deal away from the creation of wealth. I poured my heart and soul into this book. I do hope you get the most of it. I wish you the best on your journey. I wish you heartfelt success in buying one or many businesses to come. The best of Luck!

CHAPTER 1

The Small Business Space

Let's understand the small business space from a size stand point. In the United States alone, there is over 28.8 million small businesses. In Canada there's 1.65 million small businesses. In the United Kingdom, there's 5.7 million small businesses. In the rest of Europe, excluding the United Kingdom, there's 18.1 small businesses. And in Australia, there's 2.1 million small businesses. That is a total of 56.35 million small businesses just in these areas alone. Of course, this gets multiplied by the millions when you consider Latin America, different parts of Eastern Europe, Asia, Africa, New Zealand and many other regions and countries. But Just in the USA and Canada alone there's over 30 million businesses. In Europe, there's over 23 million businesses. In Australia, over 2.1 million businesses. As you can understand, the small businesses space is immense. That gives us an idea as to the opportunity of the market. Small business plays a significant role in everyday life in each economy; whether it's the United States or another country, Europe, United Kingdom, Australia, Canada, really anywhere else in the world. In all these countries, they account for more than 50-60% of the gross national product. They account for 60-70% of overall employment. By far, they are the driving force of these economies.

		Age 50-88	Age 35-49	
(millions)	# of Small Businesses	55%	28%	Age 35 +
USA	28.80	15.84	8.06	23.90
CANADA	1.65	0.91	0.46	1.37
UK	5.70	3.14	1.60	4.73
Rest of Europe	18.10	9.96	5.07	15.02
Australia	2.10	1.16	0.59	1.74
Total	56.35	30.99	15.78	46.77
U.S. Small Business Administration, UK Department for Business, Australian Small Business and Family Enterprise Ombudsman, Energy & Industrial Strategy, European Commision SME Performance Review, Canada Business Register				

Even though we see headlines in the news about the big, large companies and what they do, small businesses really are behind everyday employment and growth and purchases in any given economy around the world.

If you look at the demographics of the ownership in the United States, 55% of all small businesses are held in the age bracket 50 to 88 actually but I'm sure it goes higher than 88 years of age. This means that 55% of all small businesses, or 15.84 million, in the United States are in the hands of baby boomers. These baby boomers are retiring or close to retiring, or want to retire but having not been able to retire. And not far behind the baby boomers there's it's another 28%, in the age group of 35 to 49, or about 8 million additional small business owners will be nearing retirement age in the next 10-15 years. Ultimately, approximately 24 out of the 28.8 million small businesses or 83% of all small business in the United States are in the hands of owners that are past retirement age, are trying to retire, will soon retire or will retire in the next 10 to 15 years. This means we are witnessing and living in a time of probably the greatest transfer of business ownership in US history. This is an unprecedented and staggering occurrence.

Now, while I do not have the precise ownership demographics for Europa, Canada and Australia, we do know that they all have a larger aging population. Such just extrapolating the same percentages as in the US would be conservative to say the least. If we put all this in perspective, you have a total of 56.35 million small businesses of which 30.99 of those are owned by someone that's age 50 up to 88. And another 15.78 million small businesses that are in the hands of people that are 35 to 49 years of age. Close to 47 million of these businesses are owned by owners that are in their retirement age or will soon retire, or will be retiring in the next couple of years. Thanks in large part to global increases in life expectancy, populations in all regions of the world are expected to age dramatically in the coming decades, according to the United Nations. Europe and North America will continue to lead this trend, with the largest shares of older people through the middle of the century. This phenomenon that we are witnessing in the US is really a worldwide occurrence. There is currently and will continue to be for the foreseeable future the largest shift in ownership in modern history.

This means that it is a ripe time to be buying businesses in the small business space. Not just because of the shear amount of small businesses available, but because of the fact that they are in the hands of an aging population that will be retiring or exiting their business. We will be talking about the mindset of that population in a later chapter. Currently, there is a vast transfer of ownership happening as we speak which will continue for many decades as baby boomers continue to go into retirement in one form or another.

CHAPTER 2

Do Not Start a New Business

We know, statistics show, that 50-60% of any new business startup at fails in their first year. We know that about 80% of all small businesses fail in the first 5 years. Those are Las Vegas odds. You would have better luck or success playing Roulette in Las Vegas. These are overwhelming figures. The question then is, why would we want to roll the dice with our own money, our future, our professional career, our family's livelihood, our future legacy with worse than Las Vegas odds? This is gambling. It makes little to no sense. Yet still, over 550,000 new businesses are started every month alone in the United States.

Here is my opinion, based on 25 years of experience as to why businesses startups fail. Well, they come up with a business, product or service to sell and they think because they've done so much research and analysis that they have a winning product or service. They think that they can get it to market. They think once they get it to market, they will be able to operate successfully. Once they are able to operate, they will be able to scale the business. In doing all this make a profit and a comfortable living. But this is not what happens. Something goes wrong in one or many phases. Many things are not accounted for that rear their ugly face in the implementation.

Things are underestimated or overestimated. From paper to project to successful business there is a world of knowledge, experience trial and error that most people are not equipped to venture because of internal and external factors. This is why over 50-60% of businesses fail in the first year.

To illustrate, let's go back in time to the simple analogy when we were children and we put up a lemonade stand. We kind of know that there's a marketplace out there because if we're smart and our parents taught us well, we know to put a lemonade stand outside when it's hot and not when it's rainy or cold. I'm making that assumption that we've done our market analysis and we know that people get thirsty when it is hot and that is a good time to sell lemonade.

So we put our lemonade stand out there in the corner, with a big sign that reads lemonade for $1. And now we just sit there and we wait and wait and wait. We *hope* a lot of our neighbors and a lot of people that are driving past our lemonade stand are going to be clients. We just assume they will be because our market research told us that people are thirsty on a hot day. What really happens is some cars drive by and they don't stop or even acknowledge us. Some cars drive by and they wave but do not stop. Some cars drive by, stop and say hi and don't buy. Some cars drive by, stop and actually buy lemonade. The same can be said for people walking on the street. The market research we did told us we were going to sell lemonade. Did it not? But in reality, other than out of the kindness of people's hearts, are people really buying Lemonade because there is real demand for it? Why did all those cars that drove by and the people that walked by not buy lemonade? Do they actually want ours? What if someone puts a lemonade stand one block away, will they now buy from both of us? Did we price it correctly?

But let's assume that our lemonade is amazing so much so we run out of it. Now what do we do? From an operational standpoint, do we know how much lemonade we will need to make before we run out again? How many lemons should we buy? Where should we store them? What if they rot? Where do we source the sugar from? How do we manage the neighbors that want to buy while we figure out how to get additional raw materials to make lemonade? Where do we source the sugar and water and glasses and napkins from? Other than price what else do we need to negotiate? What if we begin to run out of sugar but still have lemons? What happens if our supplier does not deliver the water? What do we do if we mix the ingredients incorrectly and the product comes out different then the day before? What if the neighbors waiting get angry and talk bad about us? Will that affect our ability to sell lemonade in the future?

While we're at it, let's look at the finance aspect. Where do we come up with the money to buy the materials to assemble the stand? Do we really know how much money we need to put this little lemonade stand together? Do we really know how much it takes to acquire a table and chairs, to create a catchy advertisement poster, to finance the inventory of lemons, the water, the sugar, the pitchers, the glasses and the napkins? What if people don't buy any lemonade today, will we have money to operate tomorrow? And I can continue to ask hundreds of more questions regarding this and other aspects like legal issues, human resources, logistics, taxes, etc. involved in running a simple lemonade stand. What becomes clear is that putting this lemonade stand together, we have assumed that we are marketing experts, operation experts, and financial experts. Other than the kindness off people's hearts, what makes us think that that lemonade stand is going to be successful? And this is just a lemonade stand, down the street, in your neighborhood with friendly neighbors who have kind hearts. This is far from the real and ruthless business world. This is a simplistic way of underscoring that even the smallest of businesses require a lot of work and have many risks. It takes a lot more than just a great idea to run a simple little old lemonade stand on a day to day basis.

I understand that people think that starting a business is alluring, it's interesting and it's exciting. I get this. But putting your money, your professional livelihood and your family's livelihood on the line, that's a very different story. Why do we think we are so creative that the market is going to want or more importantly *needs* what we are going to offer? As much market research as we do, there is still a big void between research and reality. Are we really satisfying a need? Are we really satisfying a problem? Are we really qualified in making something that already exists better? What makes us think that we are that creative? There's existing products out there that are struggling and we think that we can improve on this by tweaking or making a product or service better. But what makes us think that we're going to convince the market to demand our improved version? I mean, let's not kid ourselves, the market will determine whether our product or service is a viable offer or not. What makes us think that we know so much about the market? The truth is that there is a world of difference and a void that we just don't know. No amount of paper research will determine how the market is going to react and in turn if you are prepared to successfully operate in it or to adjust accordingly.

But let's play devil's advocate and let's say that our product and service is accepted by the market. They see value in it. But now the question beckons, can we actually deliver this? Can we get it to market? Do we have the resources? Do we know the pricing? Will it be profitable? We've done the market research and we have determined that a particular product or service is will be accepted. Now, we have to get it to market. We have to create either a production system or a delivery system or a distribution system to get it to market. Will we open up a store front, a retail location? And where? We know location, location, location is everything. But we have studied this and found the ideal location. And now that we have found a space, we need to sign a lease and most of the time with our personal guaranty. I am sure we know everything there is to know about commercial leases. We have talked to many lawyers and understand legal contracts, even if they are 50 to 100 pages long with multiple riders. And we're going to have to remodel something existing or build something from nothing. So we have proved to be great inventors, now we are great architects and builders. No problem because I am sure we have that skillset already. And this will demand a lot of money to build out so that the product may be delivered. But I am sure we have the necessary money. And if we go the wholesale route, we need to address the same things as in retail. We'll need to lease a warehouse with personal guarantees. And whether its retail or wholesale, we need to hire our staff. We have employees lined up, trained and ready to work because we are amazing human resource managers. We have to source and manage inventory to then start selling it. Procurement is one of our strengths.

Of course I am being sarcastic. I am underscoring in a very simple manner how an entrepreneur has to get it right on so many levels to even have a glimmer of hope for success. They need to be a marketing expert, a financier, a lawyer, an architect, a builder, a salesperson, a procurement expert, a human resources manager, a real estate broker, among many other things I have left out. And we have not even opened up for business. All this is pre-opening. We have yet to enter the operating part of starting a business. And normally it is in operations, not prior, where businesses fail as execution is always flawed. The product is not delivered properly, customers complain, reviews are negative, employees quit, more money is always needed.

The question is what makes us think that we have the capability, the know-how, the experience and the expertise to deliver? But, let's continue to play devil's advocate and we are ready to open the business to the public. What happens next? Now we have to operate this business. We have to hire employees. Where do we find employees? How do we train them? What if the employees we hire that looked great on paper turn out to have issues? Do we fire them? Retrain them? Will they affect the other employees? Will they affect the clients? What makes us think that we're going to be great managers? What makes us think we're going to attract the best employees or good employees? What makes us think that we can match the training? What makes us think that we were able to train them in all aspects of the business? Are we going to be leading them or are they going to lead us? We have to find and sign contracts with suppliers. How do we get suppliers to suddenly believe in our startup? Where do we find the suppliers? What terms should we negotiate? What if the quality is incorrect? What if they do not deliver on time? Do they have the best products or are there better ones out there? How do we know? We have to find and sign contracts with clients. How do we get clients to sign long term contracts? How do we attract clients? Will they like the quality, the pricing? What if they have problems? What if they don't pay? How do we make sure we get enough clients to cover our direct costs of goods and then our fixed costs and then to even cover our cost of living? Now we have to operate all this; we have to go out there and have suppliers trust us, assure employee excellence, and complete client satisfaction. Every day all day. Not to mention dealing with landlords, dealing with tax authorities, dealing with counties, dealing with permits, dealing with competitors, dealing with maintenance issues, dealing with inventory, dealing with cash flow management, dealing with so many other things that are too many to specify that are part of day to day operations of any business.

But let's continue to play devil's advocate and assume we are able to operate. We have defied the odds making into the category of the 50-60% that make it past the first year. We are an ongoing concern. What makes us think now that we're going to be able to scale? How do we grow? How do we make it exponential? Do we have the resources? Do we have the capital? How much energy do we have to do all this? Does it have longevity? Can it last for 10 years? Can it last for 20 years?

I have started many businesses. In my early years, I started a Tequila company, an import export company, a logistics company and a night club. And a couple of years back I started a restaurant. And my overwhelming conclusion is that it is very difficult. And it is close to impossible if you don't know what you're doing, if you do not have the experience, if you do not have the capital. More importantly, if you don't know what you don't know. The business plan and market research that looks magnificent on paper is always a mere idealistic dream to the reality of starting a company. When you do a startup, no matter how beautiful that business plan looks, no matter how much detail goes behind each of the different sections; the product section, the competition section, the marketing section, the advertising section, the operations sections, the employee section, the financial section, you are going to be thrown so many curveballs. Many different things will come up that you did not plan for. That you cannot or could not foresee nor anticipate. Are you and your team really equipped for this? You have to know everything and anything about running a business. You have to be a mastermind at finances, you have to be a mastermind in sales, advertising, marketing, employee management, human resources, operations, and legal. You have to understand financial management, you have to raise money, you have to be able to do market research, you have to be able to identify your niche and understand your real clients. And then you have to package all this into a business offering that is in the ideal location, the ideal place in the ideal position for it to succeed. And this will test and challenge your startup well before any revenue is made. Startups are extremely difficult. To be successful in starting a business, you have to execute like a *fine-tuned orchestra*. A successful orchestra is one that is impeccably fine-tuned. All the various instruments are in synch, are coordinated, and always are in perfect harmony. Beautiful music comes out of a fine tuned orchestra. If one does not have a fine-tuned orchestra, a fined-tuned business, if all the "instruments" are not performing together impeccably, it will become a disaster.

What I have tried to highlight is that starting a business has a lot of risk, far too many risks in too many phases. Remember, 50-60% of businesses will fail in the first year and 80% within the first 5 years. Are you properly getting rewarded for the extraordinary level of risk? In Las Vegas, the higher the odds, the bigger the rewards. When you play the lottery, the bigger the price money, the reward, the lower the probabilities so the higher the risk of not winning. And if the business does succeed, the reward is not commensurate with the risk. For all you financial experts, there is no optimal risk reward scenario in starting a new business. The additional risk is NOT compensated with additional reward. The risk reward is unproportioned; it goes against basic economic theory. This means that even if you defy the odds and make it past the 5-year mark and are part of the 20% that did make it, there is not an additional reward for this.

So why do all of this? Why this obsession with starting a business? Why go through all this heartache of the unknown, take all these risks on where the reward is not commensurate to the risk? *The real question you should be asking, the intelligent one is, why not have somebody else take on all these risks and build it for you?* And if the business fails, it is their loss and not yours.

The intelligent path, what years of experience have taught me in the entrepreneur space is to have somebody else build it for you. Have somebody else take all these risks. Have somebody else try to piece everything together and make it all work. Have somebody else deal with all the countless moving parts and constantly changing variables in transforming an idea into an ongoing viable concern, a real business. Have someone else take all these hits, take all these lumps, sacrifice, expend the sweat, blood and tears that come with starting a business. And live with the scars over 1, 2 or 5 years until the business is stable. And once the business is up and running and it is stable, then come in and take it over. Buy it. Does that not make sense? In doing so, when you buy an existing business, everything that we have just mentioned regarding startups, all those risks are all mitigated. Somebody else took those risks and overcame them. Have somebody else build the orchestra and fine tune it until it performs seamlessly. And if that business did not survive, well, it's not for you to buy. The businesses that have survived can now be bought by you based on their cash flow. It's not going to cost you a lot more than had you started the business. *In fact, in most cases, it's going to cost you a lot less than it cost them to build it from zero.*

When you buy a business, everything you have to create and let mature is already in place. The guessing, testing and risking have been eliminated. You are buying an established infrastructure that runs smoothly and makes a profit. Employees are trained and in place. The assets and equipment are in place and producing. The market has accepted the product, the pricing and the packaging and therefore clients are consuming it. Marketing and advertising campaigns are in place attracting new clients and conserving existing ones. Supplier relationships are established, terms negotiated, and processes operating. Cash flow needs and uses are well defined and attended to. Banking relationships, taxes, permits are already in place. The business already has all the necessary elements that a viable business needs. You have a fine-tuned orchestra already producing music. All you have to do is buy it and continue to operate. You have mitigated all the risks associated with starting a business, but achieved the same outcome of being the owner of a viable business. And you do not have the scars or baggage the previous owner had. You're fresh and not beat up. You have ideas that you can bring to the table which the previous owner probably could not fix or implement because he was probably working in the business and could not see beyond each day. Running a business as a startup is especially hard and it's very difficult to get the chance to always be innovating. You now get that chance to innovate. You will be able to improve on things that the previous owner could not see. And the award is going to come to you.

This is why 10 times out of 10, I am going to buy an existing business instead of starting one. This is 25 years of experience speaking on your behalf and for your benefit.

CHAPTER 3

Do Not Start a New Franchise

Let's talk about why not to start a new franchise. We talked about why a startup is not the best alternative, in fact it is a very poor alternative to business ownership. All the various risks and challenges involved in a startup pretty much apply to starting a franchise. The main difference is that a franchise provides you with an established brand and a system for you to implement that has been tested elsewhere, whereas with a startup, you and need to create it. A franchise should provide you with processes that you don't have to create from scratch. It provides you with a product or a service that has already been successful elsewhere, but not necessarily everywhere. And they should provide you with ongoing support.

Barring this, everything else is the same as a startup. The risks are the same. You still have to find a location. You still have to build it out. You still have to attract clients. You still have to find suppliers, find employees, train everyone, launch the business and deal with operations thereafter.

While you do receive processes and manuals that provide a roadmap to launching and operating your new franchise, it is up to you to implement and execute. It really is no different than you going online and researching yourself. You can easily research how to train employees, or how to manage employees, or how to implement processes, or how to attract clients. The Franchisor is not going to be there holding your hand as you put these manuals into action. By no means does buying a franchise mitigate the risks of a startup. A franchise is a startup, just a little bit more advanced. You are able to mitigate some risks, but you're still starting from zero. The Small Business Administration has declared that franchises have the same success rates as independent small businesses. "Survival among independent businesses and franchises appears to be similar," declared economist Brian Head in the SBA's Office of Advocacy. You're hoping people will actually buy your goods and services because just as there are many successful franchisees, there's also many unsuccessful franchisees. What did one do right that the other didn't? After all, they're selling the same thing, they're using the same brand, they implemented the same processes. Ultimately it has to do with the startup risks. It could be operational, it could be managerial, it could be marketing, or it could be financial. Whatever the reason, one franchisee did it better than the other and therein lies the truth, no different than starting a new business. Starting a new franchise does not guarantee success or mitigate failure. And one could argue that it while you mitigate some things, you acquire additional challenges. With a franchise you are now less reliant on yourself then with a startup because now you have to adhere to the Franchisor's polices, rules and regulations. You have less flexibility to change directions and adapt. And trust me when I say they are not negotiable.

With a franchise, there's out-of-pocket expenses before you even start. To buy a franchise, you have to sign a Franchise Agreement, the FA, and a Franchise Disclosure Document, the FDD, which is mandated by law in the United states. This is the legal contract between you and the franchisor whereby you are now buying the right to operate their Franchise. The day you sign the FA, the Franchisor is going to ask for a franchise fee. And franchise fees can range anywhere from 10,000 to 100,000 thousand dollars. This fee now gives you the right to the brand, it gives you the right to their processes, it gives you the right to the products and services that you're going to be able to sell, it gives you the right to that ongoing support, but it all comes at a cost. Before you have even started you are out of pocket. You have already spent a significant amount of money right out of the gate. You have to consider this. You're entrusting your livelihood, your professional livelihood, your family's livelihood, your professional careers in the hands of this brand that's already costing you money upfront. You still haven't found a location in case of a retail or restaurant, you still haven't opened up an office in case of a service, yet you are already out of pocket and for some people that do not have the money, they are already in debt.

Not to mention that once the business is up and running, the Franchisor will take a royalty directly from your sales. The average royalty is about 7% on a restaurant franchise, 5% on a service franchise. Some charge as high as 10%. So you are paying for this franchise. They will take anywhere from 5 to 10% of your revenue. Not only are you out of pocket before you even started anything just by signing a piece of paper. Once you get the business up and running, once you're viable, it's going to cost you 5 to 10% for the use of the franchise. My thought process is that to pay these hefty percentages, the brand and processes and product or service must be remarkable. It must be out of this world. It must be so good that it brings in sales to not only pay for the royalty, but to make the franchisee additional profits than had they started their own business. Yet, in reality, that is seldom the case. In fact, most franchises currently operating need that extra 5 to 10% in royalty to reinvest in the business to keep it viable.

On top of this, most Franchisors will obligate you to put money into an advertising fund that they will control *for the sake of the brand.* They work the same as a royalty where they obligate you to pay a percentage of your revenues. These percentages range between 1-3%. Every franchisee has to put money into this advertising fund to strengthen the brand nationally, regionally and locally. This advertising fund should be implementing a marketing and advertising campaign that should be running ads; whether it's TV ads, radio ads, print ads, or Internet ads to give you more clients. Obviously, it doesn't work out that way for everybody because they're not running ads equally across the nation or across the region or even locally. The sad truth is that most franchisees don't benefit at all from this advertising fund. It would be better for each franchisee to put that money into their local market.

So if we do the math correctly, between the royalty and the advertising fund, a franchisee is paying the Franchisor between 6-13% of their revenues. And that is not necessarily giving the franchisee a return. It's ultimately going to the franchisor and for the franchisor's benefit. The royalty is revenues to them and they own the brand so any monies spent via the advertising fund helps their brand. So, as an intelligent reader, you can see that it costs you a lot of money to have a franchise. That's the bottom line. It doesn't mitigate all the risks of a startup, it mitigates some of them and albeit fewer of them. But it also costs you to have that brand, to have that product and services, it cost you upfront and it cost you on an ongoing basis. What do you actually get? You get manuals. Once you're up and running it's up to you to implement those manuals. And you're paying for every month. Every month you're paying to read these manuals. Every month you're paying to make the products and services. Every month you are paying to implement their processes.

Franchisors will claim that support is part of the package. You get ongoing support. Unfortunately, that's not always the case. Most franchisors give little support. They are just way over extended. And usually the support a franchisee needs is on the spot, it is immediate, it needs to be live, when the situation presents itself. And no Franchisor can react that fast, even with the best intentions. I have bought three businesses that were franchises, two of which all the franchisors did was audit us. So much for paying for support. They were more interested in making sure that our revenue records were correct and that we were paying the correct amount of royalties. The support we received was making sure we weren't cheating them. And they were connected remotely into our point of sale system so they knew exactly what our revenues were. Yet, they would still come out to audit us, as opposed to helping us, supporting us. Unfortunately, these two franchises I owned were not much different than most franchisees and their relationships with their Franchisors. Now, the third franchise we owned, the franchisor was absolutely magnificent. They would support us in any which way possible. All our questions, our doubts, new strategies, that franchisor was great. So I cannot state that all ongoing support in general is bad. But, whether it's good or it's bad, is it worth five to 10% of your revenues? That's the real question. You do have the manuals, but no one's there holding your hand and telling you how to implement them day in day out. Every single day your business is going to be presented with so many different scenarios and decisions that you're going to have to make, your employees are going to have to make that no manual alone can solve. If that additional revenue is not there, if the amazing support is not there, then it just underscores the reason why starting a franchise is not the way to go.

But for argument's sake let's assume that the support is great and the franchisor is great and even the revenue is great. Is it still good to start a franchise? Does that make the franchising a smart idea? Absolutely not. I will illustrate using the Franchise *Subway*. Pretty much everyone in the world has been to or knows about *Subway*, the sandwich company. It is ubiquitous. If there is a *Starbucks* in every block, there probably is a *Subway* almost in every corner. So let's assume two people in very similar locations bought a *Subway* franchise on the exact same day. And for argument's sake, let's assume that the cost of the franchising, the build out, the training, the materials, every cost incurred they both incurred equally. On average, per the company, the investment to start and open a *Subway* franchise costs anywhere between $105,000 to $393,000. Let's just go down the middle and say it cost these two people a total of $250,000 to build the exact same store in just two different locations. And let's assume that the size of each of the stores is the same with the exact same layout. Let's assume they both have stellar employees that are equally productive and equally effective. Their advertising and marketing campaigns are equally effective. All things considered, everything is equally the same. They've each invested $250,000 dollars to open their *Subway* franchise. And for all intents and purposes, the two franchises are exactly the same in costs, in size, in lay out, in everything. *I can guarantee that one of those Subway franchises will outperform the other. Or said another way, one of those stores will underperform the other.*

The average *Subway* makes approximately $450,000 in revenue a year according to the company. Some store sell more and some store sell less. So in our example, let's assume the better performing franchise makes $500,000 in sales and the other makes $400,000 in sales. Now let's assume both have a 10% net margin. That is their profits. After all expenses and taxes, each store yields them each 10% of the sales. This means one makes $50,000 dollars a year in profit or cash flow and the other ones makes $40,000 a year. Remember, other than the performance, everything else about both these stores is identical. Us as buyers of businesses can now go to both of these establishments and buy them. *And we will buy either one of the stores for less than the $250,000 investment they each made.*

How do I arrive at this number? That is quite straight forward and I will simplify it. When you buy a small business, in this case restaurants, you're pricing them at a multiple of cash flow or in this case net income. The multiple for small business and in particular restaurants is between 2-4 times net cash flow (we will discuss this in detail in a later chapter). If one is making $50,000 in cash flow and the other 40,000, then the first will be priced between $100,000 to $200,000 and the other will be priced between $80,000 and $160,000. That is the range that I could buy any one of these. Even if I pay top dollar for both, I will have bought one for $200,000 and the other for $160,000. However, one does the math, it will cost us less to buy anyone of these stores, *without any startup risk.*

Both took the same risk and did the exact same thing, yet one still came out worse than the other. Both of them did their market analysis. Both executed exactly as the Franchisor required them to. They both went into this journey with the same illusion, wonderment and excitement. Yet one will always outperform or underperform the other. And to me, the business acquirer, it really does not matter; it really is irrelevant. We are completely indifferent. We will buy either one or both of them at a lesser price than what they paid for. We did not waste 6 or even 12 months of our life building them and assuming all these unnecessary risks. We will let both these franchisees do that for us, and then buy their businesses at a lesser cost. We will mitigate any startup risk and the opportunity cost of building out a franchise. Both franchisees came out worse then had they just sat back and waited to buy one instead of starting one.

So I ask, why would you start a franchise? Why would you go through the headaches and all the risks of a startup? A franchise is still a startup. Why not wait for somebody else to start it, build it and then go buy it? There is no reason to start a franchise when you can buy an established one.

CHAPTER 4

Why Buying A Small Business Is Better

Why buy a small business? We know there's 28.8 million small businesses in the United States. There's 1.65 million small businesses in Canada, 5.7 million small businesses in the United Kingdom, 18.1 small businesses in the rest of Europe, and 2.1 million small businesses in Australia This gives a total of 56.35 million small businesses in these countries. And of course there are many million more in Latin America, Africa, Asia, Eastern Europe, New Zealand and other parts of the world. Small businesses are ever-present. It's a ginormous space.

		Age 50-88	Age 35-49	
(millions)	# of Small Businesses	55%	28%	Age 35 +
USA	28.80	15.84	8.06	23.90
CANADA	1.65	0.91	0.46	1.37
UK	5.70	3.14	1.60	4.73
Rest of Europe	18.10	9.96	5.07	15.02
Australia	2.10	1.16	0.59	1.74
Total	56.35	30.99	15.78	46.77
U.S. Small Business Administration, UK Department for Business, Australian Small Business and Family Enterprise Ombudsman, Energy & Industrial Strategy, European Commision SME Performance Review, Canada Business Register				

While there are 28.8 million small business in the United States, there's only 18,500 large businesses. That's why small businesses account for 99% of all businesses in the United States. This is also true in Europe and the rest of the world. A small business is usually defined by their revenue or by employees. Most sources define small businesses as $10 million in revenue or less. Other sources define them based on employees, in particular businesses having 200 employees or less. A five employee company is very different than a 200 employee company. I think this definition is tricky. For example, a restaurant that does $700,000 dollars in revenue a year has probably 25-30 because they have multiple shifts. So they may have 10 waiters for their lunch hour and then another 10 waiters for their dinner hour. Add to this the cooks, cashiers, bussers, dishwashers among other employees. When you add all your employees, you may have 25 or 30 employees although the business is only doing $700,000 in revenue. Compare this to a services company that has 10 employees. This company may have a couple of large client accounts of $3 to $4 million in revenue off of just 10 employees. So I don't like to look at the employee count because it's very difficult to gauge a business by this. I focus on the revenue. What matters is revenue and more importantly, how much profit or cash flow that revenue is producing for a given business. So going forward, our definition of a small business will be all those generating $10 million in revenue or less. My sweet spot in the small business space are businesses that are doing $7 million in revenue or less.

As mentioned, the small business space is very big. What a lot of people don't know is that buying and selling small businesses is a very active market, it is a very liquid market. I like to compare it to the residential market because it's very similar. We know there's millions of homes being bought and sold every single day across the United States, really across the world. These homes range anywhere from $50,000 to over $50 million dollars and they are being sold daily. For there to be such a liquid and fluid market, the market relies on a series of tools, middlemen, various different actors and general infrastructure in place. You have to have a lot of people that are promoting these homes to buyers and sellers and getting them out to the market. These are the brokers and realtors. You have to have capital and credit, hence a plethora of banks, lending institutions, and private investors that are actively financing these purchases. And because there's so many banking and lending institutions, you need to have mortgage brokers. As a home buyer, you have so many credit options afforded from your local bank across the street to the international banks like Bank of America or Wells Fargo, to nonbank lenders, to credit unions, to private capital or private equity or institutional funds to other lending entities. There's far too many financing options that you need a mortgage broker to guide you in finding the right program that best suits your needs.

You also have title companies. They help facilitate the transaction between the buyer and seller and assuring that title to the property, or ownership, passes smoothly from one to the other. Title companies in the United States act as the middle man in coordinating legal documents and monies while the transaction is in progress. While the buyer is obtaining financing. They assure there are no liens or encumbrances on the property so that title can cleanly pass from the seller to the buyer. Lastly, they coordinate all monies, from the deposit, to the financing, to the disbursements so that the buyer and the seller can have a smooth transaction. Lawyers also sometimes take over this function, acting as the middlemen of the transactions. I know Lawyers and public notaries perform this function elsewhere in the world. And there are many other different entities that come into play in the residential market such as home inspectors, handymen, insurance providers, home warranty services among others. This is the infrastructure in place that make the residential real estate market very liquid and hence very easy for anyone to buy and sell homes. That's why millions of homes are being sold across the United States and across the world every hour of every day. Well, the same thing is true in the buying and selling of small business.

Small businesses are bought and sold every day just like real estate. Millions of businesses are transferring hands all across the United States and across the world. Just like in the residential real estate market, there has to be an established infrastructure supporting all these sales, a highly liquid market. You have thousands of banks, financial institutions, hard money lenders, equity investors and even the government. In the United States, the Small Business Administration actively participates in credit to facilitate the buying and selling of small businesses. In fact, there are more types of funding avenues when you factor in the asset based lenders. There's equipment financing, there's real estate financing, there's inventory financing, there's accounts receivable financing, among others. You have similar types of entities and programs in the UK and many of the European countries as well as Canada and Australia and I'm sure similar entities in other parts of the world. Needless to say, there are numerous financing alternatives to facilitate the purchase of small businesses. And like the real estate market, there's many other middlemen or facilitators. There are business brokers which act the same as real estate realtors. There are title companies and lawyers that help in the transfer of ownership and title between one business owner and another business owner. They also take money and assets in escrow and legal documents, no different than a residential real estate transaction. And of course there are many other actors such as business inspectors, appraisers, insurance providers, accountants among others. All these actors are necessary for a market to perform efficiently and to make sure the market is active and liquid. What surprises many people is the fact that buying and selling small businesses is a ginormous market, and a very liquid market. There is an entire industry sustaining both. *Just like it is very easy to buy a home, it is very easy to buy a small business.*

And pricing a business is easier than one may think and you certainly do not have to be well versed in finance or business to understand this. When you look at real estate, normally you're able to tell what the price of a home is because there's a lot of comparable properties that have recently sold in the area. These homes may have been sold in the past month, three months, or even six months. One has access to this date at their fingertips via the internet or through a real estate broker. So when one is looking to buy a home, one already has a fairly good idea as to the price. If one is looking at a 3,000 square foot home with 4 bedrooms that was built 10 years ago, they will have many similar homes that were sold with these same characteristics. From these, one determines the average sales price per square foot. In our example, let's assume $200 per square foot. So the prospective buyer already knows that the home he is interested in is in the $600,000 range (i.e. 3,000 x $200). One can gauge the value of a home within a very specific range very fast because you have comparable properties that have been sold similar to the target home. The same is true with buying small businesses. The most common valuation method used to buy a small business is a multiple of cash flow. Which uses the same logic. It takes the prices that similar business has sold for, just like the homes, but instead of a price per square foot, you derive a multiple. And instead of the size of the home, you use the business's net profit or net cash flow (I will go into this in great detail in a later chapter). Suffice it to say, we are comparing business sold with the one we are looking to buy. So just like buying a home, you can very easily understand the price range of a home, you can easily gauge the price range of a small business. There's very sophisticated methods to valuing companies, and we will go into detail on these in a later chapter, but for small businesses they seldom apply.

Buying an established business will always be a better and more sound decision then starting one. You eliminate the risks of startups and a new franchise altogether. But more importantly, you are buying something that is already operating, functioning, with all the necessary elements that make a business viable. The difficult start-up work has already been done. The business has processes and procedures in place. Buying an established business means immediate cash flow. It has predictable revenue for operations, payroll, and debt service. It is not uncommon for start-ups to have to wait months to years before there is enough cash flow to cover these costs. An established business will have financial history which makes it easier to secure loans and attract investors. There is existing employees and managers with experience. They are trained and skilled, specific to the business. One will acquire existing customers, contacts, goodwill, suppliers, staff, plant, equipment and stock. The business has established suppliers and credit lines and terms. One will save on the time and effort that would be required to establish these relationships from zero and one will benefit from favorable terms negotiated by the previous owner. The business has an existing customer base and referral business. One also has licenses, permits or certifications necessary to run the business, in place. And also has easier access to credit lines, banking, and lending institutions (which we will discuss in a later chapter). Existing companies have proven track records, enabling banks to base lending decisions on actual results and not hypotheticals. Hence buying an established business just make sense.

One area that I want to explain as well is the notion of why people would sell. The skeptical theory is that the owner either wants to cash out or they sell because the business is in distress. I want to dispel both these notions as they both imply that a buyer is getting tricked or taken advantage of, and that could not be farther from the truth. There are multiple reasons why an owner will sell. In fact, we have almost an entire chapter devoted to the psychology of the business owner. In reality, most owners sell for a variety of reasons, very similar to why a homeowner may sell their home. People sell their home for a multiple of reasons that neither have or should have negative or positive connotations attached. Many homeowners sell because they are relocated by their work. Some people sell because they're going through a divorce. Some people sell because they want to downsize; their children have grown up and moved on and they would rather have a smaller home or an apartment. The same is true about a new family or newlyweds who want to start a family; they want to upgrade; they need a bigger space. So they sell to buy a bigger home. Some people do sell to cash out. They may have bought the property many years past. And some people sell because they fall into hard times and are forced to sell.

The same thing is true with small businesses. There are multiple reasons why people sell their business. They may want to retire. They are tired of their business. They have run into hardship, whether financial or personal. Or the business may have fallen into financial hardship. There may be a death of a spouse or another life altering event. And some do want to sell because they want to cash out. They have grown the business for many years and they want to now monetize this. In any event, the motivation to sell does not equate to the prospective buyer getting the short end of the stick. Quite the contrary, this is a wealth creation opportunity.

CHAPTER 5

No Experience Necessary

Why don't you need experience to buy a business? Everything about operating a business is already in place, running before you bought it and after you buy it. There are employees in place. In most cases, those employees have been there for many, many years. The employees are trained; they're running the business. There's processes in place and procedures that the employees are implementing on a day in, day out basis. Every single day the business opens and closes seamlessly with the daily challenges that any business faces, but the operations are fluid. The marketing and advertising programs are in place. Sales materials are in place. Product and services are being offered every day to customers. The price points have been established. Quality standards are being adhered to. Suppliers are in place and pricing and terms have already been negotiated. Relationships are already established with suppliers, with your clients and with your community. The reason you don't need experience is because everything is already there in spite of you. The day to day is already running. There's existing cash flow. There's existing sales. The business will not stop when you buy it. The business will continue running itself in spite of its owner. In fact, when we buy businesses, we require the existing owner to stay on through a transition period. This is very common.

The transition period assures that while there is a change of ownership, the operations and all aspects of the business continue to run seamlessly. The transition period is a time where the former owner can train the new owner. The owner will train you on all aspects of the business; not just on the managerial part or the strategic part. The former owner will also outline and highlight all those potential opportunities that now become yours that he wasn't able to capitalize on. Not only is he going to train you, he's going to guide you in making the company more efficient. Owners are very authentic about this because this is their business, this is their legacy, the business has been a part of their lives and they want it to succeed well after they have sold it. You really have to understand this. They want this business to succeed when they're gone. They don't want it to close its doors. They know the employees, they know the clients, they know the suppliers, they know the market, they know the community. Just because there's been a transfer of ownership, the sellers do not wish the company any ill will. Quite the contrary, they want it to succeed and they want their legacy to be preserved. They will do their best to help out and assure the company's viability. In as such, they will also highlight many challenges and risks and offer advice as to how to address them. During this transition period, not only will you be trained in every facet of the business, you will also be guided and things will be highlighted where you could immediately take courses of action to make this business even more profitable and the challenges so you can take immediate courses of action to address them.

For all these reasons, you really don't need experience. If you take me as an example; I've run a tequila company that we started from scratch. Trust me when I say I had no knowledge about the tequila industry, the alcohol industry, the beverages industry in general. I had no idea about packaging, starting a brand, wholesaling or retailing it, let alone manufacturing it. I had an export company that exported canned goods from Mexico to the Dominican Republic. I had no knowledge or experience in exporting from Mexico and how to import into the Dominican Republic. Not only that, I had no experience in canned products, the canned goods industry, supermarkets, food stores and food wholesalers in a different country. The same was true when we started the logistics company where we raised ten million dollars of venture capital. I had no prior experience in logistics. Why would I? Not only did I not know anything about the shipping/logistics industry, I didn't know about the industry in six different countries in Mexico, Chile, Colombia, Brazil, Argentina and United States. Yet, we were able to raise ten million dollars from venture capitalists who saw the same opportunity we saw. And we were able to open operations in 6 different countries. We hired employees to help us that did have that experience. No different than you in buying a business and having employees already in place running the day to day operations. When I bought my first restaurant, I had no idea about the restaurant industry. I'm not a cook let alone a chef. I left home when I was 14 years old and I have not lived at home since. And yet, I don't know how to cook. I can barely boil water to make pasta. Imagine me buying and operating a restaurant. I had no idea about the bar business. I had no idea about the fabrication industry. I had no idea about commercial real estate. I had no idea about burger chains. I had no idea about play areas. I had no idea about the pest control industry. I had no idea about real estate brokerages. I had no experience in an oil and gas company. I had no idea how to even measure a barrel of oil or the difference between a natural gas well and an oil well. Do you know how specialized the oil and gas industry is in terms of equipment? I was ignorant towards that. There's no reason why

I would have known about the oil and gas industry; about running an oil and gas company. When we launched a professional soccer match, I had never rented a stadium. I had no idea how to talk to a professional football club. I love soccer, but that has nothing to do with running an event. And yet it was relatively easy for me to buy and operate all these companies across multiple industries.

In all the businesses that I have been involved in over the past 25 years, in none of these business did I ever have the industry experience prior to starting or buying them. And yet I was successful. You don't need to know that business in and out in order to buy it. What you do need to understand across any business is that there's three common things, three common denominators that all successful businesses share across any industry. They are the three P's: People, Processes and Product. If you have good people, if you have good processes and if you have a good product or a good service, you're going to have a good business. And the great thing is when you buy an established business, you're going to have people, processes and products already in place. Can they be improved? Absolutely they can. And you will have that opportunity. In fact, you will be a breath of fresh air of ideas and energy to do just that. You're going to improve upon things that, with an outsider's perspective weren't so obvious to the previous owner. But the point is, there's going to be a foundation already in place. The foundation has already been laid out. The people and the processes and the product or service have already been there for many years. You do not have to reinvent the wheel. You improve on the people. You can strengthen and empower quality, key employees and get rid of bad employees. You can make the processes more efficient to increase revenue and lower expenses. You can make the product or service a higher quality at a better price point. But understand that all of these are already in place. Having experience while it's great, it is not necessary. You're going to learn how to run your business in due time. Within a couple of months, you will know that business inside and out. All that experience you thought you needed you will acquire it within a very short period of time.

You do not need experience to buy a business because the foundation is already there. The three common traits that I've seen in all of my businesses, in all of the transactions that I've been in, don't change from industry to industry. The people, processes and products or services are already in place for you when you buy a business. So Experience becomes secondary. Buying the right business with the right structure is more relevant.

CHAPTER 6

Why Do You Want to Buy a Business?

Your Objectives

It is very important for one to really understand what their overall objective for buying a business is. It's going to drive the type of business you're going to buy. There's many reasons why people buy businesses. We want to make sure and ascertain that the business you eventually buy fits your overall objective. Whether it's a short term, middle or long term objective; we want to make sure that it's aligned with where we're you want to be, where you see yourself in the future.

One of the reasons why people buy businesses is because they want to work for themselves. Currently you are probably working for somebody else and you don't have financial independence, you don't have professional independence. You are working very hard but ultimately you're not content. There's a reason why you want to leave where you are today, which has some value to you because you're there and probably have been there for some time. Most people that want to work for themselves come from a corporate job; whether it's a big company or small company they work for somebody else and they get to a point where they think, I work so hard but it's for somebody else's benefit. Now, as hard as I work, I want that work to be for myself, I want that benefit to be for my future. And this is fine.

A recent retiree may feel that he can still offer more and has skills and talents that he wants to employ. He wants to feel useful and productive. He wants to create or be a part of something. An hourly employee may feel he has more potential and has not found the right opportunity. He may be working through various paying jobs until he finds the right opportunity that fits his goals, passions, and interest.

The idea here is to really understand the driving force behind your desire to buy a business. If you want to work for yourself, does that mean that you want to buy a business and are you content with one business? Because there's a big difference between working in the business or working on the business. Working ON the business or IN the business is something you need to determine because it's very important that you understand why you're buying the business. If you're buying it because you want to work for yourself, because you want stability, because it's your dream job or your dream industry or your dream niche or you want to again break the shackles of corporate America. Those are very valid reasons and very common reasons for people to buy businesses. But that in and of itself does not determine if you ultimately want to be IN the business or ON the business.

Working In the Business

You may decide that you want to be involved in the business, the day to day operations. You may not want to be paying money to an employee that you could do yourself and make that extra compensation. This means assuming that employee's responsibilities. You may feel you can do it better or you simply want to make more money, or both. You want to relieve that expense and make sure that expense goes to you as the owner. In doing so you are now working IN the business. In doing so, you are taking on day to day operational responsibilities in the company. Whether it's marketing, whether it's finance, whether it's on the operations side, on the human resources side or sales department. You are a "hands on' owner or owner operator. Many business owners are very much involved.

Working for yourself, looking for stability, working in your dream job, and breaking the shackles of corporate America, for most people that is their end game. And these types of buyers end up working IN the business because they don't want to continue growing and buying additional businesses. They are content with a business because their objective was to break free from wherever they worked in and to gain stability or to be in the industry they've dreamed about; to have their dream job. And in this they have achieved fulfillment. This is very true for many retirees. They have worked hard, some have wealth, and they just want to be active, involved, feel productive. They don't have desires to create empires or to risk growth and expend the tireless effort to achieve it. They have already done this. They're probably going to be more IN the business running the day to day operations. This is perfectly fine. In fact, it is amazing because they have accomplished their dream.

Working ON the Business

Working ON the business means that you are involved in the strategic part of the business, you're not in the daily operations, you are guiding the business and where that business should go.

You are dealing with questions like, how do we raise sales from a strategic standpoint? How do we increase clients? Do we need to market better? Do we need to advertise? How do we establish an online presence? Having an online presence nowadays is kind of a must. You could increase sales dramatically with the right online marketing strategy. That is strategic from a marketing standpoint.

You want to be strategic from a financial standpoint. You want to look at the broader financial picture of the company. The uses and source of money. You want to hone in on those expenses where you think you could probably get either better rates from different suppliers or where you think the previous owner had been kind of careless and has accumulated expenses that are really not adding value but rather hurting the bottom line. You want to eliminate wasteful spending and optimize expenses. You could make the operation more efficient in reducing redundancies in processes, assuring employees are not overlapping in functions, making sure that there are not wasteful steps in client acquisition or supplier procurement, and developing key indexes and key points to constantly measure this. Ultimately it's a strategic vantage point in increasing sales and decreasing expenses from a financial standpoint. This leads to more profit to you or to your shareholders or to the owners of the company. All this is a strategic financial standpoint.

Strategically, you may also look at the operational lay out determine how you can optimize how things are run more seamless. You can identify where the bottlenecks are and create a more efficient operation process. If it is a fabrication shop or a factory, your physical layout could be improved dramatically by moving equipment around. You can cut down the time in your production process significantly by improving the operational flow and more importantly the process and how much it takes for machines or people to make a particular product or turn a raw material into a finished product in the various phases of the assembly line. If it's a restaurant, you may want to change the layout so that you increase capacity or you make the experience of the end consumer a better experience. You're thinking strategically from an operational standpoint. If it's a service company, you can change the service to assure the right quality of service. You can make sure that the clients are being touched as many times as they need to be touched because service is all about client satisfaction.

All of these vantage points are strategic in nature and require you being on top of the business. You are managing the strategic aspects, you're managing the future and you're guiding your business. You are not involved in the day to day affairs. You're not there from 9 to 6 or 8 to 5 or 11 to 10. This requires that you have time and you have other people, other employees, managing the day to day operations so you can guide the company to the next level.

Creating Wealth

If your objective is to create wealth or build a business empire, then you will most likely be ON the business. To create wealth with one business, you have to make it more efficient, whether it's increasing sales or lowering expenses or both. You can increase sales substantially. You can leverage marketing efforts and channels and significantly increase client's sales. You need to be very strategic and you need to invest in long term growth. You will have to hire additional personnel as your business expands, invest in equipment, machinery, and technology. And you can turn a business from a $1 million dollars in sales business to a $2 million dollars in sales company and so on. This happens all the time. This creates wealth. But it requires guided strategy, growth execution, and growing the business. You cannot be bogged down by the day to day operations. You need to control and command the bigger picture. You create more cash flow increasing sales. And this naturally leads to the overall value of the business increasing.

So how do you do this? How do you take a company and go from a million dollars to two million dollars in sales? It sounds difficult, sounds very complex, but it really isn't. Remember this, the company went from zero to a million before you bought it. This company started at one point and it is a different point today. What you need is the ability to scale the business. Now some businesses you can scale a lot easier than others. For instance, restaurants and retail stores are harder to scale by their very nature. You can increase cash flow, you can increase profitability but it's going to be very difficult to increase them by big percentages, 100% or 200%. You are inherently limited by physical capacity, by a geographic location and you're also in a very crowded space. In a restaurant, if you have 100 tickets a day, meaning 100 people are buying every day on average, it's going to be very difficult for you to suddenly have 200 or 300 daily tickets consistently. Why would twice the usual amount or three times the usual amount of people suddenly come to your restaurant? Something extraordinary had to happen for that to occur. Same is true if you're a retail store owner. If you're selling 100 products a day, it's going to be very difficult for you just start selling 300 products a day just because. You can improve advertising. You can better your marketing or the client experience. But this will render small incremental changes. These types of businesses are very difficult to scale.

To really create wealth in these type of situations is to create a brand. You're going to have to open up additional stores or restaurants. The more you open successfully, the more the brand exponentially grows in value. Not any one store in particular but the brand itself because when you create multiple profitable stores or restaurants, you become top of mind to the consumer and the intangible aspect of that is worth a lot more than having only one unit. Before it wasn't worth as much so your brand didn't really stand out, it was just your operation. Now, it's your brand, you have brand equity, you're building an intangible and somebody is going to be willing to pay a lot more for that than just a standalone business.

Now in other types of businesses, you can scale dramatically and create true wealth. Examples of these are fabrication business, a factory, Oil and Gas, auto body store, or a service provider.

Short Term VS Long Term Strategy

One of the things people do not take into account is what is the long term plan with the business they are buying? This should be factored in as it will affect your eventual exit strategy from the business. Do you want to have the business for a long time? Do you want to grow it? Or do you want to flip it? Do you want to maximize its value and then sell it? This will play a big factor in the type of business to buy. If you're passionate about a business and you're able to find the business that you're passionate about but your objective is to sell it rapidly by flipping it, your passion really is not that important and thus should not be predominant. Another factor may be steady and predictable cash flow for a long time. A business I bought back in 2009 gives me steady cash flow month in month out to this day. When I looked at this business that was an important driver and I knew I could own this long term. Do you plan on moving because of children age, weather, closer to family in the future? If so, then this needs to be taken into account as a primary objective. So, the time frame to your exit strategy is very important to define as a general objective.

In summary, you need to really understand your objective. Anything is valid. You just have to be very precise and very definitive because that's going to determine the type of business you're going to search for. You do not want to buy a business that you want to grow and be strategic only to find out that you are limited by the nature of the business or industry, or that the business operation requires you to be in the day to day operations. If you are looking to create wealth, you need to be looking at businesses that offer the opportunity to create it. And the infrastructure in place for you to be able to concentrate on the strategy and growth. On the flipside, if your goal is to run the business as status quo or with some growth and improvements, you want to make sure you fit in from a day to day, that there is space for your involvement and that you are not buying a business that needs to grow for survival sake or because of client demand or employee expectation, which will directly clash with your real objective.

Deal Specification

Buying a business can change your life. You will experience a life transformation. You have a right to be as selective as you want. As such, you have a right to find the business that is ideal for your objectives, for your lifestyle, for your overall professional and personal goals. You're in a position where you can find your ideal business. There's a lot of criteria that needs to be defined to determine what your ideal business is. How important is a life work balance relationship? How much time are you going to devote to the business? How much time with your family? Is travel important? Do that you have certain experience in certain sectors? Do you want to "flip" the business? Is there a specific industry or sub industry that interests you more? This is a time for you to look at all these and other factors and understand what you really want in a business. There's millions of business out there. They're all over the United States, Canada, Europe, Australia, and the rest of the world. You can't go after every business. You have to be specific. The more you know what you want, the more specific it can be and the more guided your deal sourcing will be. Sit down and begin to define these based on the following minimum criteria:

Industry

What industry do you want to be in? Buying a restaurant is very different than buying a landscaping company, or a steel fabrication plant, or a retail store. And within restaurants, buying a fast food restaurant is different than buying a fine dining restaurant, as buying and Italian restaurant is different to buying a Bakery. In the following table is a list of industries and subindustries that BizBuySell.com offers as categories as a guide:

- Accounting and Tax Practices
- Agriculture
- All Non-Classifiable Establishments
- Architecture and Engineering Firms
- Art Galleries
- Assisted Living and Nursing Homes
- Auto Repair and Service Shops
- Auto, Boat and Aircraft
- Automotive and Boat
- Bakeries
- Banking and Loans
- Banquet Halls
- Bars, Pubs and Taverns
- Beauty and Personal Care
- Bed and Breakfasts
- Bike Shops
- Bowling Alleys
- Breweries
- Building and Construction
- Building Material and Hardware Stores
- Business Real Estate For Lease
- Business Real Estate For Sale
- Campgrounds and RV Parks
- Car Dealerships
- Car Washes
- Casinos
- Catering Companies
- Cell Phone and Computer Repair and Services
- Check Cashing
- Chemical and Related products
- Chinese Restaurants
- Cleaning Businesses
- Clothing and Accessory Stores
- Clothing and Fabric
- Coffee Shops and Cafes
- Commercial Laundry
- Communication and Media
- Concrete
- Convenience Stores
- Dance, Pilates and Yoga
- Day Care and Child Care Centers
- Delis and Sandwich Shops
- Dental Practices
- Diners
- Dog Daycare and Boarding
- Dollar Stores
- Donut Shops
- Dry Cleaners
- Durable Goods
- Education and Children
- Electrical and Mechanical
- Electronic and Electrical Equipment
- Energy and Petroleum
- Entertainment and Recreation
- Equipment Rental and Dealers
- Financial Services
- Flower Shops
- Food and Related products
- Food and Restaurants
- Food Trucks
- Funeral Homes
- Furniture and Fixtures
- Furniture and Furnishings Stores
- Gas Stations
- Glass, Stone and Concrete
- Golf Courses and Services
- Graphic and Web Design
- Greenhouses
- Grocery Stores and Supermarkets
- Gyms and Fitness Centers
- Hair Salons and Barber Shops
- Health Care and Fitness
- Health Food and Nutrition
- Heavy Construction
- Home Health Care
- Hotels
- HVAC Businesses
- Ice Cream and Frozen Yogurt Shops
- Indian Restaurants
- Industrial and Commercial Machinery
- Insurance Agencies
- IT and Software Services
- Italian Restaurants
- Jewelry Stores
- Juice Bars
- Junk and Salvage Yards
- Landscaping and Yard Services
- Laundromats and Coin Laundry
- Legal Services and Law Firms
- Limo and Passenger Transportation
- Liquor Stores
- Locksmith
- Lumber and Wood Products
- Machine Shops and Tools
- Magazines and Newspapers
- Manufacturing
- Marinas and Fishing
- Marine/Boat Service and Dealers
- Massage
- Medical Billing
- Medical Devices and Products
- Medical Practices
- Metal Products
- Mexican Restaurants
- Mining
- Mobile Home Parks
- Motels
- Moving and Shipping
- Nail Salons
- Nightclubs and Theaters
- Non-classifiable Establishments
- Nondurable Goods
- Nursery and Garden Centers
- Online and Technology
- Packaging
- Paper and Printing
- Pawn Shops
- Pest Control
- Pet Grooming
- Pet Services
- Pet Store and Supplies
- Pharmacies
- Pizza Restaurants
- Plumbing
- Preschools
- Production Companies
- Property Management
- Real Estate
- Retail
- Routes
- Rubber and Plastic Products
- Schools
- Security
- Service Businesses
- Signs
- Smoke Shops
- Software and App Companies
- Spas
- Staffing Agencies
- Storage Facilities and Warehouses
- Sushi and Japanese Restaurants
- Tanning Salons
- Thai Restaurants
- Towing Companies
- Transportation and Storage
- Travel
- Travel Agencies
- Tree Farms and Orchards
- Truck Stops
- Trucking Companies
- Vending Machines
- Vineyards and Wineries
- Waste Management and Recycling
- Websites and Ecommerce
- Wholesale and Distributors

Size

This is a question I get often: How big of a company should I buy? There is no right answer to this. You can buy a $500,000 revenue business as well as a $5-million-dollar revenue business. It comes down to your comfort zone and your capabilities. Some people want to start large while some people small. But you do need to define this as the infrastructure, the processes, employees, clientele for a $500,000 revenue business will be very different than a $2 million revenue business and a $2 million revenue business will be different then a $5 million revenue business. The larger the business is, the more institutionalized it will be. The larger ones generally have more seasoned employees and more seasoned processes, and products and a more established infrastructure in place than smaller businesses. But they are more complex, have many more moving parts, are relatively more expensive and harder to buy. A smaller business has less employees and less processes. The owners are more accessible and the price may be more advantageous. And they are all in all simpler. But they required to be more hands on in the operations.

Location

Location should not be taken lightly as it can affect other criteria. Do you want it to be near you where your drive is 10 minutes? Can you drive an hour across town? Do you want it in the same metro area where you live? Do you have children? Do you have to be home at a certain time? Is travel a factor? Can you live in New York and operate a business in Miami? You have the ability of buying a business very close to your home and at the same time you can buy a business that's thousands of miles away. I have friends who have businesses in different countries and that is normal. I've had businesses in different countries as

I mentioned before; there's travel involved and that is something you have to factor in. Do you want to relocate and buy a business in a different city, state or even country? Many people use the purchase of a business to relocate to another location that they have dreamed of living in. Conversely, many people are willing to relocate to buy the ideal business, the business of their dreams.

Absentee

There's a lot of what are called absentee run businesses. Absentee means that the owner is generally absent from the business. The owner could take a three-month vacation and the business will still run itself. You can have a business that is not necessarily one that you have to go to on a daily basis and hence be limited to a geographical area. Now, you have to be in contact, it is your investment at the end of the day. You have to know how to supervise it and analyze it and be constantly on top of it. It also means you are probably going to pay a premium for this luxury. The price will take into account an owner's salary or compensation to operate the business. Now a manager will be taking this compensation so that the owner can be absent. Also, these business are harder to find. And you really need to determine if the business is truly absentee. I have a country western bar that I bought in 2009 that I have been to a total of 10 times at most, and some of those times were to enjoy a good night out. The managers of the business send us periodic reporting and we have strong systems in place. But I am absent from the business operations. The business does not depend on me.

Working IN or ON the business

We talked about this in the Objectives section so I'm not going to go into it here at length. When you analyze businesses, the type of business may require you to be more involved than another one will. If the business is in distress, then you're going to have to be there to turn it around. You are going to have to be there every day. If marketing could be improved, you probably have to spearhead that. If there's growth potential and that's why you're buying it, then you're probably going to be involved as well. All of that will force you to work in the business. However, if there's a stable, strong management and key employees in place and the systems are running great then you can work on the business and take it to wherever you want strategically. You'll have the time to implement new growth strategies, marketing initiatives, personnel changes and any other value driven initiatives.

Passion

Wouldn't it be the greatest thing in the world if your passion can be in the business you bought. For example, I am an avid soccer player. I love soccer. I play soccer four or five times a week and have been playing it all my life. Wouldn't it be great if I could own something that has to do with this passion of mine? Buy a soccer team or a youth league or indoor soccer facility. This is an example of how one can combine their passion, their hobby, their love of something with a company to buy. But of course, this is a lot harder as you are substantially limiting your business prospects. This is an objective that I have yet to fulfill and hopefully will fulfill in the future. But if you love to cook then buying a restaurant is very feasible. Or if you love to work out, then buying a fitness gym is very doable. The more passionate you are about something, the more it is great to wake up every day and go to work. So if you can match your passion with the business you're buying, then then all power to you.

Expertise

Your business expertise may help you in deciding which business is a better fit. If you are well versed in finance maybe an accounting company or financial advisory or a business consulting company will suit you. If you have been in marketing for a long time, you could buy an online marketing company, or you can buy a company whose marketing activities are very important to the success of the business. If you have operational expertise maybe a factory or a wholesale business will be a better fit as not everyone can handle complex machinery or specialized labor. Do you have a specific trade such as being an engineer or a lawyer? If so, you can buy a law firm or an engineering company or you can buy consulting company where law or engineering is an important part of it. Architects can buy a home remodeling company. There are many skillsets and expertise and businesses that can very easily accommodate these or complement one another.

The Life-Work Balance

The Life-work scenario is a very personal one and may trump all the aforementioned criteria. Is it important for you today to have a balance between your personal life and your professional life? Only you can answer that. There are people that are workaholics and they work 60 to 80 hours a week and don't distinguish between a weekday and a weekend. Their professional life is part of their personal life. There's other people that want to work from 9-5 and go home and completely disconnect. Time with their family, with their parents, with their friends, with their pet is important to them. You have to find a business that allows you to live the life you chose to live. If you buy a business in another State, you're going to have to travel and that's going to be part of that decision as it will affect your personal life. How important is your availability to your family? Do you want to be absent from the business? Do you want to work full time? These are life balance equation type decisions that only you and you can decide. Also know that if your idea is to create wealth by growing the business or by buying many additional business, this will require extensive amount of hard work, dedication, and sacrifice for many years. You need to factor this as well from a life-work balance perspective.

Now, a word of warning. The more specific you are, the less deals you are going to ultimately see. If you're too specific on the exact industry, size, location, and balanced lifestyle between professional and personal, the amount of businesses available will be limited. You will have less business alternatives out there to go after. You have to learn how to prioritize and give certain criteria more weight and relevance than others. You can still be as close to your ideal business as possible. But you don't want to be so limited that you're constantly looking for that perfect business that is elusive and that is very hard to find. This can lead you down to a very frustrating path of never finding the *right* business. The more specific your criteria are the more limited your sourcing capabilities and you're targeting.

Nonetheless, this is the time for you to find the business you want. You're in a privileged position where you can idealize what that business would be, your ideal business and try as much as you can to come close to finding it. Just make sure that you put the right importance on the factors that you deem to be important and not so much importance on the factors that aren't as important as others. So prioritize. You're going to have to spread your net wide, cast your net very wide to find that specific business. But make sure it is in the direction you want to be.

CHAPTER 7

Types of Sellers We Target

We know that small businesses sell for all kinds of reasons. There isn't one general reason why a business is for sale. We know that there is an abundant supply of small businesses out there. There are literally millions of small businesses spread out throughout the United States, Europe, Australia, Canada and the rest of the world of course. What kind of business owners are we looking for? The ideal business is to buy something that is at a reasonable price, that is a good business to buy, and then you could buy with zero or very little money down. What types of businesses fit this profile? Pretty much any business fits this profile. However, there's two particular types of business owner that makes finding this type of business structure easier and these are the types of sellers that we look for. The first is the baby boomers, the older, retired or soon to be retired business owners. And the second is the Multi Business Owner.

Seller Profiles

Seller Profile – The Retiree

If you recall from the previous chapter, we talked about over 56 million small businesses that are active. We also mentioned that about 83% of them were owned by people that were 35 years old or higher. In fact, 55% of the businesses in the United States were aged 50 and up. For more than half of the business in the United States, the business owner is in the second part of his life and has already entered into retirement age, he's right at the cusp of retirement age, or in the next 5 to 10 years will enter retirement age. It does not mean they will retire. It means that retirement and entering the next phase of their life is ever present. The populations in Europe, Canada and Australia are older populations compared to the United States. These figures as a percentage of all the small businesses in those various different countries is even more pronounced; which means the market for small business with this age demographic is bigger from a percentage standpoint.

In this age group, everybody around these business owners has some sort of exit plan or has already executed one. They already have a retirement plan in place, a dream that they've been thinking about all their lives. I've been thinking about my retirement and I am only 47 years old. I've still many years ahead of me but you can't help to think that one day you want to stop working. The baby boomers are the biggest generation of our time. In the United States, the majority of business owners are baby boomers. They're in this retirement age and that state of mind. And so you have the majority of small businesses out there that are owned by this demographic that is in the frame of mind of exiting the business. That's important, that's the key. They already see themselves out of the business. Whether that's tomorrow or five years ago or five years from now, they have been thinking about this for quite some time. In fact, they have already retired in their mind, it is crystal clear. It just hasn't materialized in real life.

The mentality of these sellers is to sell, to exit. They may not have done anything to get to that stage. But in their mind they have already decided to exit the business. In their mind they have a plan in place already to sell the company, to inherit the company, or to close the company. What exactly that plan entails may not be entirely crystal clear. But make no mistake about it; an exit strategy is already in the horizon. Exiting the business is predominant in their psyche, it's predominant in their everyday decisions in the business, it's predominant in their lack of moving the business forward. It has permeated the business and the business culture and the business is probably more stagnant than it is alive, because decisions aren't being made with growth potential, or rejuvenation, or with fresh ideas. The motivation of the owner is not there anymore. They are already thinking about exiting. We will analyze their psychology here shortly.

This is the type of business owner that we target. This is the type of seller that we want to deal with. This is the type of seller that is more amicable and amenable to doing a more flexible, structured deal. They value other things then just cash at closing. They're willing to do owner finance. They're willing to entertain other structures that typically other buyers that are not in this mindset are less flexible on. I would say that approximately 80% of the businesses we want to look at are in this realm; with these type of owners. This is by far the market segment that will allow the purchase of a business where you will risk no money. As the statistics unwarily prove, fortunately, these businesses and business owners abound.

Seller Profile – The Multi Business Owner

The other type of business owner we want to concentrate on is the multi business owner; the business owner that has multiple businesses. And there are many investors that fit this description. Even I fit this description. Recently, I had a conversation with a person that owns over 650 restaurants. He is one of the bigger restaurant owners in the United States. He started looking to buy restaurants from home. He was not a restauranteur or a chef. He was looking and searching and he had a big plan and a big idea on how to get funding and he bought his first restaurant. He's perfected this method. But he started from his house with no experience and now owns 650 restaurants. This type of owner is selling restaurants all the time. And not all those restaurants that he is selling are going to be greatly priced or priced to his benefit. He wants to sell them quick. He prefers to sell them then having to deal with them because he doesn't have the infrastructure to supervise so many businesses. He has a manager and infrastructure in place at each restaurant. However, he has 8 staff members at the corporate level supervises all aspects of owning 650 businesses. Needless to say they are severely spread thin. Sometimes it's costlier to have too many businesses. We look for these types of owners, because they are more amicable to better structures, better terms, not much more different than large real estate investors. There's a lot of real estate investors out there that own hundreds of homes; of all shapes and colors and these type of investors are willing to finance the sale of most homes. And it's not much different with these large business owners. They are willing to do more flexible terms, do owner financing, do structures that are more sophisticated and not your everyday cookie cutter, black and white buy-sell transaction, which is what the business brokers like to do. In fact, the buys businesses very similar to how we buy businesses. They do not risk their own capital and buy businesses in industries that they don’t have any previous experience in. They understand our objectives and will help in achieving them. These type of business owner we want to target for the type of deals that we're looking for.

Seller Profile – Business Broker

Then there is the third type of Seller which are those that list their business for sale through a business broker. And these are the last deals that we want to look at. This is going to be surprising to a lot of you. Business brokers are priming sellers to a win-lose situation and also a lose-lose situation. Later on in this chapter, we'll talk about the psychology of the business broker and why you should buy from them as a last resort.

Psychology of the Seller

Remember, approximately 24 out of the 28.8 million, or 83% of all small business in the United States are in the hands of owners that are past retirement age, will soon retire, are trying to retire, or will retire in this demographic. So if you recall, more than 80% of the business we want to target have owners in their later years. They are baby boomers that have reached an age where retirement surrounds them in one way or another. This type of seller thinks and acts in a very specific way. It thoroughly important to understand why we are targeting this demographic because it is the target market that has the highest probability of affording us the opportunity to buy a business without risking our own money. The hypothesis of this book is centered around this. For this, we need to be thoroughly familiar with the psychology of this type of business owner. And 80% of the reasons for these sellers to sell are NOT 100% cash at closing.

I want to stress that when I use the word retirement, I use that word very broadly because these business owners are far from retired. They are just in an age or in a phase in their lives where their mindset already has an exit plan. Whether they've implemented it or not is not that relevant. This set of owners already have an exit in mind for the business. This is by far the biggest group that we want to target in terms of business owners because they want to or have already exited the business in their mind. They are on "Exit Mode". It means that they have internal and subconscious motivations to sell. Their psyche is motivated to sell and when you're motivated to do something, you don't need a lot of arm wrestling or a lot of convincing to get to that point. In fact, as a prospective buyer, you will bring a lot of relief to a lot of these owners because you will help get them to that exit. You will help get them to the objective of leaving the business and going to the next phase in their lives whatever that may be.

By no means am implying opportunism or a win-lose relationship or scenario. When a seller is motivated he is more willing to deal with you, he is more open to structures that he might not have open to had his mindset been different. He is more flexible in terms and structure. To highlight this, let's look at it from a different perspective. You have just purchased a business. You are so excited. You're going to grow this business. You're going to make it more efficient. You're going to create wealth. You've gained financial freedom. You've gained professional independence. You've broken the corporate chains that have held you back for so long. You have a renewed sense of self-confidence and self-purpose. Your mindset is on the business and its prospects. Imagine if somebody came up to you after you bought that business and offered to buy it. You would probably thank the person and kindly say "No Way"! You're not there, you're not open to it, you're completely closed off from it. In fact, you are 180 degrees from selling, you're completely in the opposite direction. You're going forward, the buyers asking you go in reverse. You're at the prime of being a business owner, you're just beginning. You are an unmotivated seller. This is what we mean by mindset. The business owner we are targeting is motivated. His mindset is there and it is aligned with your interest. Subconsciously, he wants to sell. He just hasn't put a "for sale" sign up anywhere.

Burnt Out

In conjunction with the demographic of this target market, there are many reasons at play that are behind this mindset to retire or exit the business. The most common that I have seen is that they are burnt out. It just natural. They have been probably working in this business for many, many years. Many of these sellers have been working in his business for most of their lives and for some, all of their professional lives. And they are exhausted. They're just done. The business has consumed a big part of their lives for such a long time. It's very simple to understand. They've had enough of that business and they've reached an age where frustration comes easier. They get overwhelmed easier. They have less energy which further feeds into the burnout. They want to start the next phase of their life. They are eager to move on.

Health Issues

Other circumstances also play a role. They become sick more often. They have health issues. They are in or are entering an age that illness unfortunately becomes a part of life, a reality. They have to attend to health issues more frequently and this interferes with the business. Or the business begins to interfere with their life. Or maybe it's not them. It may be their spouse or siblings, or their friends. They're in a phase of their life's where health issues tend to take over and the business isn't as important. The business becomes secondary. I hate to say this but it's true, they're in in the process of dying. As they age, their friends or family members are dying or have died. And this is transcendental. They are aware that they have fewer years left then before. And they need to live them fully. Many times not having the business becomes a big source of relief for these sellers.

Run Out of Ideas

Some have simply run out of ideas. Most of these business have probably been stagnant for many, many years. They have probably not been open to new ideas because the owner is set in his ways. They started these businesses years ago, sometimes 10, 20, or 30 years ago when they were pioneers. When they started these businesses they were fresh. They had big ideas and hopes. They had immeasurable enthusiasm and the technology they implemented surely was cutting edge. But today, they're probably behind and have simply run out of ideas. At some point they stopped progressing. They have not evolved. Or they have simply been unable to keep up. They are stagnant. We see this not only in business, we see this in in our personal lives with our parents, we see this with our older friends, with our grandparents, it just happens. If you think about the Internet and ecommerce, this demographic has been the last to adapt. Most of them don't have Facebook, Instagram or Twitter accounts. Email is still a struggle. Think about how difficult it is to teach somebody that doesn't have a Facebook account how vital Facebook is as an advertising platform. Or someone that still uses the yellow pages the importance of positioning and placement in google searches. These things simply do not register to them. Hence, they've run out of ideas. What worked when they started simply just does not apply today. And the truth is, they know that their business or certain parts of it are stagnant and will be so long as they continue operating.

And this means that they cannot keep up with their employees, technology, or the competition. A lot of their employees want to implement new things that the owners cannot keep up with or don't understand. And now they're constantly fighting with change. Change is being forced upon them by their own infrastructure, by their employees, their clients, their suppliers or even their competitors. Even as they're interviewing new employees. They are not understanding or don't want to understand a lot of the ideas that these new employees can bring to the table and don't hire them. They have run out of ideas and every day now is a struggle. Every day is a disagreement. Every day is conflict because even though they want to run the business; they are falling behind. This leads to frustration with their employees as they recognize change is needed. This affects their clients that are demanding new standards that competitors are offering. And this affects the morale and affects the culture. They are already behind in the business and that is a day to day struggle for them. They recognize this but resist because change implies the unknown. And it is ultimately their business and their pride as well. Every day, something happens to remind them that they are keeping the business back in some form or another. This is a silent truth they will never admit outright, but that they know all too well. This is a day to day external and internal struggle.

No Succession Plan

Many of these owners don't have a formal succession plan. The Millennials, the newer generation, may not want to take over Dad's Plumbing Company. They don't want to take over mom's flower shop. They don't want to take over their parent's wholesale food company or furniture distributor. They want to do something different. In fact, they are probably already working in a corporate job or are working on a business online or some new technology. Some have started or want to start a new business (they obviously have not read this book). Whatever the case may be, in the majority of instances, there is no succession plan. The only succession plan that they have is to close the business. Many business owners end up doing just that. They close the doors and go out of business. To me that's unfathomable. How would I let my business close? It's a business that is generating money, it's a business that is generating cash flow. How can I just turn that off? How can I just unplug that? Again, you have to get into their mindset, not my mindset or your mindset. They have already exited. They have already reaped many benefits through many, many years with the business they now have. If they have no one to give this business to, or nobody wants this business, they would much rather close it, get relief and move on. They're not necessarily looking to monetize the business. It's easier just to shut it down.

Some Cannot Close

In most cases, they will not close down the business even if they want to. it's their legacy. It is what should survive them in some form. Their legacy needs to be preserved. So they begrudgingly push forward. For others, it may cost money to close down the business. It may be extremely costly to just shut down. They may have payables, they may have taxes, or lease obligations with the landlord, guaranteed by them personally with many years still left on the lease. They may have bank loans. They may owe the bank or other financial institutions money and closing down the business makes them incur have to pay these in full. And mind you, they are at an age where they're not as productive as they were in years past and so, any of these costs will directly eat at their retirement savings. These expenses will directly affect the next phase of their lives. And so they can't close. They keep on struggling every single day. Although in their mind they've already closed, but they can't actually close because they may incur all these costs. Some would rather give away the business to bypass these costs. They'll give it away for a dollar. This happens often. They're not really giving it away for a dollar because someone's assuming those liabilities, but they are relieving themselves of a potential cost.

Some sellers will not close because they have a strong sense of loyalty to their employees, to their clients, to their suppliers and to their community. It's a strong emotional time in their lives to part ways with something that's been equally or more important to them than their personal life. They spend more time at this business than anywhere else they have throughout their life and they can't just leave. It's their name on the door, it's their legacy. The business itself is their legacy. Their employees, their clients, their suppliers and community is their legacy. That's probably one of the reasons why they haven't sold it in so many years, because of their loyalty to all these actors. They are worried about who will take care of them if they are not there. Of course, they will all survive and be just fine. But in the owner's mind these are their people, their community. They have a long lasting deep bond and relationship. And the owner wants to protect them. One way of doing that is to keep the business going, in spite of their own wishes.

Fear of Competition

Some sellers in this target market will not list their business with a broker because they fear competition. They tend to distrust more. Because they have a lot of experience they have probably been burnt once or twice. It happens in business all the time. Someone's wronged you or various people have wronged you. As you grow older you gain experience, you become more skeptical of people's intentions. You tend to question a lot of people's motives. We know this of elderly people that they're less trusting. Change to them is difficult. Trusting new people is difficult. They will not list their business with a business broker because they're worried, they're afraid that prospective buyers will steal their clients, steal their employees, steal their suppliers, steal their ideas. Whether that's true or not is completely irrelevant. It is very true to them and it's very real to them. Hence, they will not list their business with a business broker because they're afraid of the competition. They feel that people will use their knowledge and compete against them.

Instability

Some think that if they begin a "sales process", they're worried that their employees might find out and instability will creep in. And this can lead to losing their employees. They don't want to hire new employees. Remember, they've already checked out. They don't have the motivation to start hiring new people, to start building new relationships, to start building trust with new employees, especially key employees. So losing employees or the fear that instability may creep if the employees know that the business is for sale, again, is very real and very scary for them. They are sacred that they may lose clients. Clients will begin to leave them and go with somebody else because they may not get the same service or the same product. Suppliers may reduce their terms. They have been working with suppliers for many years, even decades. And a lot terms that were agreed to were on a handshake or on a promise, a verbal agreement. Now they fear their suppliers are going to second guess whether any of these agreements are going to be held up. This is a fear for the owner. It's not so much that any of this will happen. It's the fear that these business owners have that that it may or can happen.

Competitors unfortunately do prey on this. Competitors sometimes do disguise themselves as potential buyers to steal parts of a business. That happens, not often but it does. That is why you need to sign Non-disclosure agreements before you visit businesses to try to prevent things like this from happening. Unfortunately, they are very hard to enforce. And it's difficult to detect it immediately if somebody does this. This does happen and it scares these owners to death. To this type of business owner this is dire.

All in all, this is psychology. All of these variables one way or another play into the psychology, the psyche of this type of business owner. That's why we target this business owner because they are already wanting to sell, they just may have not expressly stated it. So as business buyers, we can make it a win-win situation. We can buy it in terms that are amicable to both parties. I want to stress it is in no way opportunistic or predatory. That is not the strategy. If somebody interprets that through this book, I want to be crystal clear it has nothing to do with predatory or opportunistic motives. It just has to do with finding a win-win solution where you can buy a business, at a good price, without putting money down. And where the seller is able to sell their business and move on to the next phase of their life's. Somebody want to sell and somebody wants to buy. If you are able to position yourself as someone that is going to carry on their legacy, then, psychologically speaking, it's an even a bigger win for them than it is for you. They will be prouder and happier for it. In fact, they will be regular customers and regular mentors of yours.

Carl Allen who is a well renowned business buyer throughout the world did a survey as to the motivations behind a Seller's reason to sell. I don't have the pleasure of meeting him as the writing of this book. I believe he's based out of Europe. The survey boils down to this: 80% of them say that cash at closing is not the primary reason for selling;

- 45% of them say the number one reason why they sell is to make sure that their business falls in safe hands to continue their legacy.

- 18% say to safeguard their employees.

- 15% just want some kind of cash at closing.

- 10% want relief and retirement.

- 6% eventually want cash, but not necessarily at the closing.

80% state that the motivation behind why they sell is not a cash deal. I can't stress enough how important it is that we understand the psychology of this demographic. While we may not agree with it. While we may think differently, it doesn't matter, it's very real to them. We can buy the business that we want on amicable terms, add a structure that we think is flexible and where we do not risk any of our money and where the seller's very content. It becomes a win-win situation.

Psychology of the Business Broker.

One of the last places we want to look for businesses are those businesses that are listed for sale by business brokers. There are many reasons why. To understand this is to understand how the business brokerage industry works and the psychology of the business broker. The business broker does not get paid on an hourly basis, on a monthly or weekly basis or a retainer. They get paid the same way a real estate agent gets paid, by commission based on the sales price of the business. Naturally, most brokers want to sell a business for a bigger price; it's natural, it's normal. There thought process is: *If I could sell a business for 800,000 dollars that's worth 600,000 dollars, I'm going to make a commission on 200,000 dollars more than I would have, had I sold it for less.* Business brokers make 10% commission in the United States and I believe it's the same elsewhere, although, I do hear that some business brokerage commissions structures are different in Europe. In certain countries, some are lower in the 8% range and some higher in the 12% range. In the United States, the average is 1%. If there's real estate attached to the business, it's 6 % of the sales price of the real estate. If you're selling a business that has real estate, the broker in the United States will make 16%; 10% on the business and 6% on the real estate. It's just natural for a business broker to want to have a business priced more so on the high end then on the lower end.

We need to also understand how business brokers obtain their clients. This is critical to understanding the psychology and overall relationship with the broker and their clients, the seller. Most of their clients are obtained through prospecting and through traditional cold calling. They're either sending fliers, making telephone calls or knocking on doors and visiting the businesses unsolicited. And they are asking the businesses if they would ever consider to sell their business. They execute a very thorough presentation as to what the selling process is and how they can help the business owner maximize the value of the business and get top dollar for it. They claim they understand the buyer mentality and they will be representing them and their best interests. They're being honest. I don't question the integrity or the honesty of the business broker. They are making a living at their craft and the majority of them are honest professionals and they do a good job. The problem is that it's at odds with real market price and it distorts the real market value is of the business. Remember, they are "selling" to the business owner. Part of that sale is increasing expectations to get the deal. They also have to somehow make up for the 10% commission the seller will ultimately pay. So inherently the business is already more than 10% mispriced. Unfortunately, those expectations are inflated and do not reflect the real market value of the business.

Like anybody else in the commission space, they want to have as many listings as possible to sell as many businesses as they can, to make as much commissions possible. They know that the majority of their listings take a long time to sell and some will not sell. So the more listings they have, the more the probability of some of those selling. It is ultimately a numbers game for them. Prospecting is how 90% business owners become clients. The business broker is actively soliciting the business. And the biggest selling point, the most important part of their sales pitch is that they can get them top price for the business and 100% cash at closing. This is really the most compelling reason from turning a cold prospect into a client. Albeit, this starts a frustrating process of raising expectations of value above true market reality.

The reason why I try to avoid buying businesses brokers, if possible, is that they convince the seller of a valuation that is just unrealistic. They inflate a valuation and misguide the seller on the actual price of the business. These guys are not corporate financiers. They didn't come from a mergers and acquisitions background. They're not investment bankers. They're not business appraisers. Some may be, but the general business brokers out there are not. They have never done complex deals. The business broker is just facilitating a transaction. He's a middle man. There's a big difference between sophisticated investment bankers who know how to value companies and come from that background; dealmakers who are in the business of structuring deals across industries, from people that just put buyers and sellers together and guide the transaction. Yet, they set the expectation of the seller's price higher than the market normally would pay. And there is no creativity in the deal structure. Usually just a cash deal or conventional owner financing or bank financing with cash. They are not versed or trained on more sophisticated deal structures.

They came up with this term seller's discretionary cash flow (SDC) or owners benefit, which at first I didn't really understand. To calculate SDC, they start adding certain expenses back to the net income. Expenses such as the seller's salary, the sellers phone expense, the seller's insurance policy, the seller's vehicle expense, the sellers travel expense. The premise is that these are not business expenses, rather benefits to the owner. Some are normal and understandable. But most of the time there are some very questionable add backs. They are called add backs because they were already subtracted from the income in the expense section and now they're being added back to arrive at the SDE. Now the that is used to value the company is higher because of all these expenses that are being added back. And most small businesses are valued based on a multiple of earnings. So if you have net income of $100,000 and SDE of $200,000, and you apply a 3X multiple, the valuation of the first is $300,000 vs the SDE valuation of $600,000. There is an immediate bias towards the seller to add back as many expenses possible to get a higher valuation for the company.

The explanation behind this practice is that those expenses would not be in there and they are only being run through the business to reduce taxes. They are really personal expenses. My perspective is that if they are business related expenses, they are business related expenses independent of who benefited from them. If they are necessary to run the business, then they are business expenses and should not be added back. Whether the expenses belong to the owner, or the manager or the wife or the sister, it's still an expense to the business. That said, if they're trying to lower their tax burden and they put their groceries in income statement, that I understand. I understand that those are in the income statement to show more expenses and lower their income to pay less taxes. I've seen this many times where owners run their personal expenses through the income statement. I can understand adding those expenses back because it's pretty black and white that they're not business related expenses. But in reality, and in practice, there are a lot of grey zone in these so called add backs. Expenses that are not so easy to identify by the prospective buyer because he does not know the business as well as the seller. And often times many of these add backs turn out to be business related. But the buyer finds this out often too late or after the fact and has already paid a higher price as a result.

To further exacerbate things, the business broker will seek a higher valuation because they apply a higher multiple from the onset. If we're using the 2 to 4 multiple range, they'll probably value the business on the upper range of the multiple, using 3.5 or 4 X, and they'll convince the seller that their business is worth it. They'll justify value by playing on the owner's ego to get their business. They'll highlight how they've been in business for so long, the longevity of the company, the infrastructure, the strong client base, the strong supplier base, the consistency in their earnings for many years, etc. They're creating a value in the seller's mind that is unrealistic. Not only are they increasing earnings with questionable add backs, they're applying a higher multiple than the market normally would allow. Some naïve or first time buyers will pay for that, unfortunately. When you add a higher earnings number and a higher multiple together, naturally the valuation will be increasingly above market value. It is artificially more expensive.

The consequence of this is that the seller has bought into higher earnings, a higher multiple and thus a higher value. And bringing a seller down to reality in terms of valuation is very difficult. Let's look at the psychology of what has occurred. They were not thinking about selling until they were convinced by the business broker, in an unsolicited manner. The most compelling reason to sell is that they will receive top selling price. So only if they receive top price are they willing to sell a business they had no intention of selling. And now that it is listed for sale, they've already spent that money in their mind. They have started traveling. They've already bought a car they never considered buying. They probably bought a better house or built an addition to the house or paid off their mortgage. In their mind, they have already spent that money. Psychologically speaking, it is a deadly exercise to spend money you don't have. When that money does not materialize, your dreams are shattered, because you have already spent the money in your mind. As a buyer, when we make them an offer that is lower than they expected, it will never meet their expectations. The lower offer alters their dreams, their future, their plans. The offer is pretty much deal dead on arrival. Sellers will just not come down from their inflated price.

What the business broker has done is create an environment where the seller is in a lose-lose scenario. The probability of the seller selling at that price is very low, yet the seller will now hold out as much as possible for that sales price and structure. *This inevitably prolongs the sale of the business.* And the sad reality is that most of these businesses don't sell. In fact, the statistics are staggering: only about 15 to 20% of all listed business sell in the first year. For every for every 10 deals that a broker has at any given time, only 1 or at the most 2 of those will sell in an entire year. The remaining 8 or 9 business owners who have been spending this money in their head are still operating their businesses one year later. The business brokers are bringing prospective buyers, but the business hasn't sold. And here's another staggering statistic that just underscores the reality: 75% of the remaining businesses that are listed never sell. That is astonishing. 15-20% sell in the first year and out of the 80% remaining, 75% of those never sell. As you can see, the business broker is playing a numbers game. The more listing he has, the more probability that he's going to get sales. Yet for the majority of the business owners, their businesses won't sell because they're artificially priced too high, the expectations are set too high. Those expectations lead to an unrealistic understanding of the value of the business in the seller's mind that he will not come down from. This exemplifies the lose-lose situation. They could have sold the business months if not years ago priced it to market.

Most business owners never come down even if the offers are fair offers. I am monitoring their listings because every once in a while a good deal is available. But what I really look for are listings that are aged, that are already passed the one-year mark. Why? Because the sellers now are motivated. The sellers are frustrated. The seller wants to sell. They have been wanting to sell since the broker came and knocked on the door way back when they were prospecting years back. Time is now our best ally. If he was not motivated to sell before, now he is. His exit strategy is fading. He is more motivated and he's frustrated. His business has been in a sort of stagnation. If one is selling their company, are they going to invest in the business? Are they going to hire new employees and deal with loyalty and start new relationships? Are they going to invest in new machinery? Are they going to get the needed maintenance on their vehicles, equipment or machinery that you normally would have? No you're not, you're going to postpone this because why wouldn't you? They will postpone all this. Now, a year later or maybe more, they have to address what they have naturally postponed. They have to *return back into* the business, financially, psychologically and in many instances physically. As a result, they are more frustrated than ever and they want to sell. And they really want to get out because they don't want that exit strategy, which they have bought into, to slip away. They don't want to keep putting off costs and investments and having to change their mindset into operating the business because they were already in "sell mode". They are frustrated and they're very motivated to sell.

Now the business broker is receiving these frustrated calls with heightened frequency. The business broker now has to deal with angry clients. The business broker has to deal with this frustration. He hears time and time and again, "you told me this was going to sell", "you gave me this sales pitch", "you told me I was going to sell at top price and nothing has happened" ... "I want to sell my business". He's hearing this not from one but from multiple sellers. That's the nature of being a business broker. You deal with happy and you deal with frustrated sellers. It's just the nature of their business. No different than a real estate broker where they deal with happy sellers whose homes were sold fast and they deal with not so happy sellers have not sold in quite some time. It's the nature of their job. But this part of the job wears anyone down. Even though it comes with the territory of being a business broker and working on commission, it doesn't mean that it doesn't agitate them. It does not mean that they're not frustrated. When you get these calls with such frequency, it wears on you. So now the business broker is motivated to sell. He's now essentially doing a 180 degree turn on the seller and telling the seller: *the only way we can sell now is we're going to have to bring the price down. We've already tested the market and the market did not accept the previous price or structure. We are going to have to be more flexible in price and the structure itself. I've brought you many different buyers that had offers but you chose not to accept them.* He didn't say, I gave you the original valuation. Rather, he says, you chose not to accept the offers. And he's right. The seller chose not to accept those offers. Anything will sell at the right price. Businesses will sell, it's just a question of price. Now, the business broker is telling the seller to lower the price, to be more flexible in the structure, to be more amicable with the buyers and while the seller hates to hear this, he knows he has to because he's already been through this journey for many months if not years. If he wants to truly exit he needs to change his price and structure.

This is where we enjoy working and dealing with business brokers. They have aged listings that have very little resistance from their clients in general. Sometimes they will even forego the "qualifying" process just to get more buyers in front of the seller. When they first got that listing, the business broker would qualify all buyers. That's what they told the seller: *I'm going to bring you qualified buyers, buyers that I know can close on this deal. I'm not going to waste your time with unqualified buyers because it's wasting everybody's time.* They qualify buyers by making them fill out buyer questionnaires, a non-disclosure agreement (NDA) and by making them send proof of funds. All of this is done at the very beginning of the listing. That's just normal operating procedures. Whether a listing is active for one day or for one year or three years, the business brokers should be doing this as a matter of process. Now the business broker may skip these steps, the NDA, the buyer's questionnaire even the proof of funds. They are now motivated in getting more buyers. For a buyer, it becomes easier to get to the seller and a motivated seller that is. The broker begins to play for the buyer and not for the seller who's his client just to get the deal done. If he gets the deal done, he gets his commission and he gets the frustrated seller off his back. He is now looking for good buyers who can make a deal. And this plays right up our alley and this plays right into our strengths.

That's why we would look at these type of listings, the aged listings. The valuations are now coming back to market. Where they should have been from the start. They were before artificially priced out of the market, they're now coming back to market. The irony of all of this is had we knocked on that seller's door as opposed to a business brokers knocking on the door, we probably would have come to an amicable deal and a win-win situation months if not years back. The seller would have gone his merry way, happy, and we would have taken the business to where we want to take it. This is the reason why I tend not to use business brokers until I have to. Only in the very few instances where the listings are aged and now the business broker and the seller are in the right frame of mind, the mindset that I need them to be, or where they should have been all along.

CHAPTER 8

Finding the Business to Buy

To really find the ideal business and not risk your own money, you have to have multiple different efforts for sourcing deals all at the same time. The more you have, the higher the probability. The easy way is to go to a business broker or go on a listing site and find businesses. But more likely than not, these will not be an ideal business based on your deal specifications, or they will require some money on your end. That is fine. But if you are looking for your ideal business where you can leverage the business assets and the owner without putting up any capital of your own, then you are going to have to work hard at finding these deals. We are looking for a business whose owner can give us more flexible structure to the deal to achieve this goal. And that means multiple sourcing strategies at any one time, and in each strategy, having multiple businesses to analyze. Essentially, this is a numbers game. To find your ideal business, we're not going down the traditional path of looking for listed companies for sale. We may go and get listed deals as the first deal we buy. The structure may not be ideal, or the price may be higher, or it may not fit your dream deal specifications. That said, I have worked with business brokers in the past. The good deals, the ones I favor, are few and far between with them. Whatever sourcing mechanism we implement, we need to understand this is a numbers game. It is imperative that you have multiple sourcing strategies in place at any one time because if we look at it from a funnel standpoint, you're going to be analyzing tens if not hundreds of to find the right one.

You're looking for the ideal business and structure. You want to make sure that the deal, the business you end up buying has the best structure in place for your benefit. Ideally, this is one with no money down from you. It is in the industry that you want. It is the size that you want. It is in the location that you want. It can benefit from the skill sets that you have. It has an established infrastructure. The business has longevity and has been around for a while. And it has good management or an employee base in place. The only way to achieve this is to have multiple sources and multiple deals being sourced at any one time. That takes a lot of hard work, yet it's very achievable, it's very doable. That's what the deal makers do on a day to day basis. I go through probably 10 businesses a day or at least analyze on the surface ten deals a day to see if any one of those deals merits additional attention and has the beginnings of what could end up being a business to purchase. Anything that I do not like, I immediately discard and go on to the next business. From sourcing to buying a deal, a lot has to happen. If we look at it from a numbers perspective, for any number of businesses we are looking at any one time, expect probably about 25% of those deals to make it past the first phase. So by definition the first phase would be scrutinizing and filtering deals to meet your deal specifications. If a business meets the majority of the criteria that you laid out in the deal specification, then they go to phase two. If not, you discard them immediately and continue to source for additional businesses.

Phase 1 will be looking at deals on the surface; the industry, the location, the cash flow, the size. Most of these deals will be scrutinized on paper, although some will be when you reach out directly to the businesses themselves.

Phase two would be meeting with owners and trying to get the owners to come up, to agree with your deal. Now, during this meeting remember, you are doing the investigating, you are going to discard many businesses at this phase.

Phase 3 will be making an offer and having that offer being accepted by the owner

Phase 4 will be negotiating and closing the deal.

Normally, if you have a hundred businesses, 25% of those deals should meet the majority of your deal specifications. Out of those 25 deals, probably about 50% of those will make it to Phase 2 where you're meeting the owner (we will talk about this in a later Chapter). Now, you're meeting 12-13 owners and their businesses in more depth. Approximately 65-70% of these business you will discard as you obtain additional information you did not like or the owner has discarded you as a potential buyer. So 3-4 business will make it to phase 3 where you are sending them a Letter of Intent, an offer to purchase. Out of these, only about 50% will ultimately accept the Letter of Intent. This will now be phase 4 where you enter due diligence, negotiations and eventually a purchase. So that is 1-2 business out of 100 that have a chance of being bought to the specifications of your ideal deal structure. And even at this stage, there is still a probability that you may not buy one of these as some deals do fall apart in the final stages as the lawyers now involved cannot make it work from a legal standpoint. This is the reason why you need to have constant sourcing of businesses through the sourcing mechanism that we'll talk about here shortly.

The more deals you have sourced, the higher the probability of you buying your ideal business. Remember, this is not emotional, it isn't personal. Deals fall apart at any one of the four phases. That is ok. You just pick up and move on to the next deal. This should not be an emotional process. There's numerous reasons why any deal can fall apart. Keep the momentum going day in, day out. This is an everyday, constant effort. There needs to always be momentum. You choose how much time you want to put into it. But again, it is a numbers game. The harder you work at this stage; the better results you will ultimately obtain.

I would recommend that you spend the least amount of time on the depth of any business. This is really the stage where you're analyzing businesses on paper. And you just want to make sure that you concentrate on the ones that you like the most. Filter them fast with your rigid criteria, with your deal specification list. Look at 5 to 10 a day and immediately discard the businesses that are not ideal for you. As you enter Phase 2 and you meet the seller, give yourself time. Do not jump to conclusions or make rash first impressions. Many buyers make this mistakes and within 10 to 20 minutes of meeting the seller, they have already determined if this is a good deal or not. And many miss out on good deals. They tend to not like the facilities. Or something about numbers was not to their liking. Or they may get scared of the complexity. Give it time. Be open minded and objective throughout the meeting. That said, you should really have a good gut feeling after your first meeting with the seller. If you are leaning more negatively, do not expend more time or resources on additional information or meetings. Move on to the next one. Also, at this phase, be wary of sellers that are not committed to selling. Some sellers will just waste your time. It happens very little, but it does happen and so move on. You want to be able to recognize this and pass quickly and not waste your time because you do not want to get down to Phase 3 or even Phase 4 where you've already have financing in place, where you've already done due diligence which can be very time intensive and then realize that the seller never wanted to sell in the first place.

Another word of advice as you are sourcing deals, in particular in the first 2 phases; do not get desperate or frustrated. That could be the difference between buying a good business or making a bad deal. A lot of times, we are so enthusiastic about buying a business and making a deal that we tend to force it. Bypassing a lot of these steps, bypassing your deal specification, not doing your due diligence correctly because you want to get the deal done. This may get you in a business you do not want to be in. Do not let desperation, frustration, or emotion force you into a deal that you would otherwise would not do.

Remember, as you go through these different phases, be very, very cognizant of the seller's state of mind and the sellers emotional state of being. While this is a business transaction to you, this means more to the seller. While you need to be unemotional, understand that this is a very emotional process for the seller. For most of these sellers, this will be the only time in their lifetime that they sell a business. And to many of them, they're not just selling a business, they are selling their baby, they're selling their legacy, they are selling their life's work. It could lead to seller's remorse where they may want to back out of the deal. You have to be empathetic. Understand that this is a very emotional journey for the seller and always positioned yourself as that person that's going to take the business to the next level. That the business is now going into trusted hands, it's going to someone that can make sure the legacy survives, that the employees are taking care of, that the clients are going to continue to receive good service. All of these things you need to constantly reaffirm back to the seller to ease all this emotional turmoil that he is going through. He is selling a big part of his life; a big part of his history.

Direct Approach

By far, the best and most effective way to ultimately acquire the business that you want, your ideal business, is through the various direct approach methods that do not involve a middle man. As previously mentioned buying a business is a numbers game. This does take time. It takes tenacity. It takes perseverance and it takes a dedicated work ethic to get to that ultimate business you're going to buy. Direct approach means that you're proactively looking for businesses that are not for listed for sale. We talked about the mentality, the mindset of the seller that we are targeting. He is already looking to sell. In his mind, he is already in an exit strategy mode. He wants to get out, he wants that exit and get into the next phase of his life. That said, he has not sold his business. It is not listed with a business broker. He is still operating the business. Your job is to find these types of sellers.

You need to go directly to the source, to the owner. This is not easy, by any means. It is very difficult. But doing it right and doing it again and again, every day, day in, day out with a systematic approach will optimize your ability to get a deal done.

Direct Prospecting

The first approach in the direct approach is cold calling business owners. This, out of all of the approaches is the most effective, but also the hardest. This means you pick up the phone and you call businesses that you have identified. You go and visit businesses that you have identified. You establish a direct contact or connection; a human connection via the phone or visiting the owner. You have to know which businesses to visit. You have to do your research. Your deal specification is your guide. You need to know whether you want to buy a restaurant, whether you want to buy a fabrication facility, whether you want to buy a pest control company, whether you want to buy dry cleaners or you want to buy a retail outfit, whether you want to buy a distributor, and so on. Your deal specification is so important because this is where we're going to put that criteria to work.

Your deal specifications will help you identify all those possible businesses that you can directly prospect. This is as direct an approach as it gets. But it works and it is effective. Put together a database of target companies. This part is key. The quality of your results will depend on the quality of your data. So if you are trying to buy Coffee shops/Cafe's in the US, use all of the usual methods: google searches, "list of coffee shops in the (your location)"), try to find online databases, visit the coffee industry association websites and extract the list of their members. In other words, do your research thoroughly. Once you have these businesses identified, whether by telephone or in person you will need to pitch yourself. You may need to get passed the gatekeepers, all those employees that will be between you and the owner. And you have to be creative in doing so. So you will need a script, something to say to the gatekeepers and eventually to the owner himself.

Below is an example of a pitch to get past the gatekeeper for the Coffee shop/Cafe example:

“Hi, it’s John from "X" (your investment group name here). We are a retail Investor group who make investments in Coffee shops/Cafe's, I'd like to have a chat with the Owner of the (business name), can you put me through, please?"

If they ask for more information, note that you need to speak to these people in simple language. Your objective is to simply get them to put you through to the owner, or provide his/her details. Say something to this effect: "We are considering investing capital in your business to help upgrade everything, or potentially become a part owner subject to us checking a few things. I'm just being careful because this is a sensitive discussion, do you think you can just put me through to the owner?"

Eventually you will find a way to get passed the gatekeeper and now it's time to pitch to the owner. Owners are suspicious, you need to move very slowly, you need to warm them up. I use two different scripts.

"Hi (owner name here), I am calling from X (your investment group name here), we're a Coffee Shop/Cafe investment group. We are looking to make investments in the sector. I am calling because we wanted to have an exploratory conversation with you to see if we could start a dialogue with you. Our mandate is quite flexible and allows us to discuss making partial investments, all the way through to 100% acquisition when applicable. Once again, we are very flexible and want to initially have an exploratory conversation.

A second script is more direct:

"Hi, my name is Joe. I have been observing and I'm a big fan of your business and I would like to explore the idea of me buying your business from you. Now, this may not be top of mind to you but I like your business and I think that I could add value to it and more importantly, I can offer you a structure whereby you will be very content on the actual purchase of the business. Is this of interest to you?

Another technique that I have not used but is used by a colleague of mine that has also bough many business is the following and I will quote him verbatim;

"So, the key to any sales situation is positioning. We want to always be the Judge and not the Judged. We decide if the business is an investment/acquisition candidate. The Business owner needs to sell us on choosing them. How do you do that? Well, this technique isn't for the faint of heart. But it only takes a little gut to implement. Get your business list and prepare to call. If you get a Gatekeeper, you say:

"Hello, I saw your business on (however you found them) and we're looking for the best "whatever biz" in the "whatever area" to invest in. Does "Owner name" handle those types of matters? (If you don't have owner's name, you can ask 'Who would I talk to about potential investment in the company?) Great, I've got a few minutes right now, is he/she available?

If so... proceed...

Hello "Owner First Name", our investment group is looking for the best "whatever biz" in the "whatever area" to invest in... who would you recommend we contact? (99.9% of the time, they will say they are the best). Oh wow, that's awesome. So, tell me, what makes you the best?

(This has to be said with some finesse lest you come off as a jerk. They will typically try to qualify themselves if you've done this right though)

Repeat back what they said makes them the best. From here, you can move into your other criteria questions if you like. I, however simply say, "This sounds good. We're talking with a few owners and will be making a decision pretty quickly. How soon could we take a look at the current financial picture of the company?" This gets me to the financials conversation without needing to say it. They will usually ask, what do you need and I list the needed docs. The goal is to have them trying to qualify for your investment (which may turn into acquisition instead) and you have much more compliance if you deliver this correctly. Whenever I tell someone what I'm doing, I say I'm looking for good qualified businesses to invest in or acquire. I typically get much better referrals."

Whatever script you use, the end game is to start a process of communication. That's how you get a conversation going; whether it's via the phone or whether it's going directly to a business. The owner will probably be taking aback; he will be surprised. He may not know what to say. He may even feel a bit overwhelmed and this is normal. Not every day do people come in and knock on your door and say "I want to buy your business". It's a very positive thing because you are now validating his business and more importantly, you're validating and immediately making them believe that that exit strategy that is in their mindset can finally materialize. But you will get rejected, you will get ignored and potentially even hung up on. Just keep at it, and the deal flow will come. Remember, this is a game of numbers. Always opt to speak to the owner first, always meet them face to face when you can. Buying a business is done via relationships, they need to be able to trust you and your intentions. There is nothing sexy about cold calling, but this is the reality of how proprietary deal flow can be a built. And getting past the gatekeepers is the key challenge here. You will normally be speaking with a low-level employee. Think about it from their point of view. If you are calling, and you sound credible, and you let them know that you are from an investment group who can invest money and upgrade the business, they will be more excited/inclined to successfully connect you through to the owner.

Social Media

Another approach in the direct approach is leveraging the power of social media. You want to make yourself very present in Facebook and LinkedIn primarily. As a precursor to this, make sure your Facebook page and your LinkedIn profile are showing you in the best light. Make sure you are presentable and are seen as a serious, respected professional. If you do have a profile on Facebook or LinkedIn, make sure that you tidy it up because it's going to be the first impression you make on prospective business owners when they see you online or somebody that will ultimately present you to a prospective business owner. If you do not have a profile on Facebook or LinkedIn, then make a profile. Position yourself as a professional, as a serious person and someone that is in the deal making or buying businesses, consulting or entrepreneur space. You will be scrutinized by potential owners when you reach out to them or any middlemen that will eventually introduce you to a potential business owner. So anything you need to do to improve your profile that positions yourself as a serious deal maker or entrepreneur, now is the time to do it.

On your Facebook and LinkedIn profile post to your network, to your current network. You are going to be surprised by the response. You post the following or something to this effect:

I am actively looking for a business to buy and you'd specify in what niche you want to buy that business in. If you're looking for a restaurant you would say, I'm actively looking to purchase a restaurant in x location. if anybody is interested in selling or if you know of anybody that may be interested in selling, please reach out to me directly. I very much appreciate it. Thank You.

That's it. That is what you would post to your network. These are to your friends, family and the network that you already have in these two social media platforms. It's very simple, it's straight and to the point. It is designed to be very direct and very succinct. Be prepared for people to respond immediately.

Now, let's take this a little bit further; in Facebook there are multiple different groups. These are pages in these social media platforms that work more like a membership or a private group that have all convened around a common interest such as running or cycling or cooking or retirement or vacationing or entrepreneurship or small business management or in fact, buying and selling businesses. Go into Facebook and start looking for groups that are aligned to the niche or industry that you're looking for or that have common interests or just small business owner or entrepreneurs. I suggest you start with any of these. You're going to be surprised as to the amount of different pages and groups that have members that are all interested in that subject. Most of these groups are private so you will have to join. You will ask to join and in a short amount of times you should be accepted. The same thing applies to LinkedIn. In LinkedIn, they have these same groups formed around a particular subject or interest; entrepreneurs, deal makers, small business owners among many other interest. Or the industry or niche you want to buy the business in. You have to do a lot of searches and researching to make sure that you're going into the right groups that are aligned to the interests of the industry that you want to buy. Once you've identified these groups and pages within Facebook and LinkedIn, then you want to introduce yourself and do the exact same thing that you did in your personal network. You're going to want to post the exact same thing, but this time, you're just going to introduce yourself:

I am John Smith and I am actively looking to purchase a business in Y niche in this X location, again, if any of you are interested or if you know of anybody that you think may be interested, please contact me privately. I thank you in advance for reading this. Sincerely, John Smith.

Email

Another direct approach is to actively e-mail people. It's no different than what you're doing in LinkedIn and Facebook, but it is now direct and targeted. You're going to find out who the owners are, you're going to these businesses websites that you want to target. In Google, there's so many ways you can extract emails from many websites so that you can obtain people's e-mails. You're going to e-mail the business owner or people in the business. Try to make sure that it's the business owner because you do not want to raise any red flags unnecessarily with employees and you also want to avoid the gatekeepers if at all possible. In that email, you're going to put templates that follow here shortly. This is a numbers game. You're going to be sending numerous of these e-mails to very directed and targeted businesses that you want to buy.

Direct Mail

Lastly in the direct approach method direct mail. This is what I call the black envelope approach. You're going to buy a black envelope, you can buy them at OfficeMax, Office Depot, Staples or any office supply retailer or online. Why a black envelope? Because it stands out. In that black envelope, you are going to send a letter and that letter is also going to be printed on a black piece of paper. And you're going to have to write this template that follows below, no different than the e-mail template, is just going to be in mail form. You're going to HANDWRITE out the letter, the owner's name and address, your name and address and you're going to put a physical stamp on it so it doesn't look like it's mass produced or it's mass labeled, it needs to appear like it's a personalized letter to somebody. The key here is that it's black so that it stands out from all the other mail. These businesses receive lots of mail and they tend to throw out all the garbage or they have gatekeepers that do this for them. If they get a black envelope, it's going to be different than what they receive every day. When they see that it's personally written and there's a hand written personal return and it has a real stamp, the gatekeepers or the owner, will think it is a personal piece of mail. That's the whole point of having a black envelope on a black piece of paper and a handwritten note in the envelope. It is to ultimately draw the owner's attention. The open ratio is higher than all the other mail that they receive. If you do this tried and proven method, the success of them opening your envelope as opposed to the other 10 or 15 pieces of mail that they receive every single day is going to be higher. Some of them are going to like it and some of them are going to hate it, but they're going to open it and that's ultimately what you want.

Here's two templates that can be applied to emails and letters. One is a short form and is more generic. The second is more customized based on your specific research of a business target.

This is the short form email and or letter:

Mr. John Smith,

You've probably receive lots of letters, phone calls and contacts from brokers, investment bankers, competitors, accountants and deal makers, this is different.

I'm an entrepreneur backed by a number of prominent investors and private equity groups who is looking to purchase and run one company. If you're ever thinking about exiting from your business and want to explore a quick, flexible transaction, please call or email. My information is below.

Thank you,

Adam Doe

Tel: +1-617-254-3256

25 Boylston St

Boston, MA 02116

Here is an example of a more customized email or letter:

Mr. John Smith,

Congratulations on the company celebrating its 25-year anniversary. I am sure that 25 years ago, you never could have imagined that today the company would service over x amount of client, in x amount of states. As the company is a leading player in the X niche sector, I am sure you probably receive a lot of letters, phone calls and contacts from brokers, investment bankers, competitors, accountants and dealmakers who are looking to turn a quick profit, but who have no idea about you or the needs of your company.

This letter is quite different because I am an energetic entrepreneur with a long term focus, looking to purchase and run one great company. I am backed by a number of operators and investors. I have work experience in sales, internet marketing and brand positioning. I also have a college degree in Business Administration from Boston College or program, and a backing of a number of prominent investors and equity groups are additional reasons we will build on the success you have had to date.

If you're thinking about exiting from your business and are interested in and exploring a quick flexible, transaction, please call me at your number, or email me at your email *adamdoe@gmail.com. Thank you in advance for your kind consideration.*

Thank you,

Adam Doe

Tel: +1-617-254-3256

25 Boylston St

Boston, MA 02116

These are two templates for emails and letters in the direct approach method.

You always want to follow up with a phone call. No different to what we talked about before. This time you're going to say *Dear (Owner's Name) I hope you received the letter I sent you. Is this a good time to speak?* You want to get them on the phone and start a conversation. They may make reference to the envelope. If they do, you say, *you are a busy man and I needed a creative way to get your attention. Now that I have your attention, I would like to make you this business proposition. Hopefully you will be amicable to it.* Then you start talking about the possibility of buying the business.

Those are the various direct approach methods. This method is all about establishing rapport and getting that business owner to start looking and contemplating the possibility of a prospective buyer and selling their business. Apply these approaches on a daily basis. This is a numbers game and the more sources that you have, the more likelihood you have of buying the business you want.

Personal Network

Buying a business is a transformation. It is a life altering event. If ever there was a moment to leverage your personal network, this is it. This is when you should reach out to all your friends, acquaintances, and colleagues. The more people you reach out to, the wider you your net is cast. They can, on your behalf, reach out as to their networks. It becomes a snow ball effect in your favor. Start making calls to your friends, and say:

Hello (Joe, Jenny), I am looking to buy a business in (niche), do you know anybody that may want to sell? Can you also put a post out on Facebook or LinkedIn to your network on my behalf? Can you send e-mails to your contact list saying "I've got a good friend, he is looking to buy a business in this niche, if anybody is interested or knows of anyone that could be interested, please reach out to me so I can reach out to him and put you guys in contact".

Your friends will help. Your family as well. This is a time to reach out to your brothers and sisters, to your cousins, aunts and uncles, your brothers and sisters in laws. Your friends and family they will be more than happy to help you in buying a business. Your individual efforts with regard to social media could be exponentially increased by the help of your immediate network. You're really not asking for a big favor here. Buying businesses has a certain sex appeal, a coolness. And people naturally like gravitate to this. They like to attach themselves to these types of efforts. Imagine the power if all your brothers and sisters, your parents, aunts and uncles, your cousins, your brothers and sisters in law, your in-laws, all in some way or other put a post on LinkedIn and Facebook and sent out emails to their networks. The result is exponential.

Extended Network

You want to do the same with your extended network of professionals. All the lawyers, accountants, insurance agents, financial advisors that you know. These professionals in particular are always dealing with business owners. Many times, they're sitting on deals, they are privy to the information. But they don't have a mandate to do anything with it. But they know business owners that have been talking about selling, they know business owners that may be going through a rough time personally, they know business owners whose businesses may be struggling, where you can add value. You are giving them a mandate to ask.

Contact other professionals in their field. So you're not cold calling lawyers, accountants, financial advisers. You're asking for referrals from professionals that know you. You need to leverage your professional network. All of these have insight into their clients. Contact your doctors and dentist. They are constantly having casual conversations and you have just given them a talking point. Most people have long, established relationships with their doctor and dentist and so informal conversations are common. Have them work on your behalf. You just put in the filler out there saying; *hey Dr. Smith, I'm looking to buy a business, if you happen to know of anybody that is selling a business in this niche, please let me know because I'm actively looking*. They will be more than happy to help you. Do not underestimate the power of using your professional or extended network. All of these people have their own personal and professional networks and you can leverage that and the effect is rampant.

Internet Sites

Most internet sites will have businesses for sale posted by business brokers. While we've already talked about how business brokers have given the seller unrealistic expectations, they still have good businesses and there could still be deals to be made. Craigslist.com has a mix of listings by business brokers as well as the owners themselves. Many owners that want to sell their business without a business broker use Craigslist to sell their businesses. These are owners looking to sell their business because 1) they don't trust the business brokers, 2) they may want to control the process, 3) they're very nervous or anxious about competition, 4) they may be going through financial distress or 5) they simply don't want to pay the commission. Craigslist is now ever present in most parts of the world certainly very present in the U.K. and in the United States. These are business owners that have already made the decision to sell. Three other sites that I like to use is www.bizbuysell.com, www.bizquest.com and www.businessesforsale.com. The latter one has a bigger presence in the Europe, while the first two are very strong in the United States. All have a presence almost worldwide. This is where we start getting into the business broker sphere. Most of the listings in these sites are business brokers listing these companies. However, there are a few business owners that are listing through these sites. It's just very hard to weed out the private sellers from the business brokers. Like these websites, there are many others. You just go to Google and search business for sale and multiple websites will appear.

Business Brokers

Lastly you have the business brokers. Like I said, it's probably the last resort. Don't get me wrong, they add a lot of value in the process. It's just a harder way to get the ideal deal done. It's a numbers game here with the business brokers because they have trained the seller to think in a very unrealistic matter for the type of deal that we can get. That said, business brokers abound. The majority of small business sales are done through business brokers. There's thousands of business brokers in the United Sates, the UK, Canada, Europe and Australia. There's local business brokers that work in your city or town, there's regional business brokers and there's national and international business brokers. They come in all colors, shapes, and sizes. There are some business brokers that are international, that have local chapters or local franchises. Sunbelt business brokers is an example of one of them. Transworld business brokers is another one. Empire business brokers is another one that comes to mind. But, while these and others national business brokers have a local presence, you will find that most business brokers tend to be more local than regional or national. If you live in Chicago and you look up business brokers the majority are going to be only Chicago-based. If you search for business brokers in Miami, a lot of the business brokers you saw in Chicago, barring the national ones, will not appear. The ones that will are local business brokers in Miami. And some business brokers specialize in certain industries. You have business brokers that only deal with restaurants, others that only deal with pest control companies, and others that may only deal with bars.

A good business broker will have multiple listings. Many of these listings are not necessarily listed on the internet websites that I mentioned, the multiple listing services. They tend to list a some of their listings but certainly not all of their listings. Naturally, they will tend to list the ones that are going to sell the most. Why? Because listing in these multiple listing services websites like the ones I mentioned cost money and so they want to use the ones that they know they're going to get a return on their money. All of their listings should be listed on their own company website.

In their website, you will see all those aged listings that we talked about, the ones that have not sold for six months, a year, two years or longer. In the business brokers' websites, you will see that the listings are numbered. They have a number like 5240. So as a tip, the latest listing is usually the one with the last number. So 5240 would be the most recent listing. So in this example, if you see one that has the 5009, well, that's certainly been there for a long time because there's been over a two hundred and thirty listings after that. Call the business broker and find out how they list their businesses. They will be more than happy to tell you. At the end of the day, they want to make a transaction and they want to work with a willing buyer. Certainly, reach out to the business brokers and pick their brains and use them. Specify what type of deal you want, in what industry, the size, whether it's absentee or semi absentee operated, whether the seller will accept owner financing. The business brokers in this respect could be of great value to you. While they may try to push their individual listings, they will still look to ultimately make a transaction.

Because there's so much to know about a business, not all the individual brokers know about every single individual listing that that broker may have. And what I've come to understand is that their commission is normally not shared. Whereas in a real estate transaction, if there's a 6% commission charge to the seller, normally, there's going to be two real estate agents involved and they will split the commission. That is very true in the United States and I know that's very true in Europe and in the UK. And I'm sure it holds true in most countries the percentage split may vary but they do share the commission with other realtors. In the business broker world, that is not necessarily the case. If you have business broker A and you have been dealing with business broker B, and you come across a listing that is business broker A's listing, business broker B will probably not be able to help you. You would have to establish a relationship with a business broker A. This certainly makes it harder and it forces you to work with many business brokers at any one time. In most cases you need to find and talk to the listing agent, the listing broker that actually has that listing.

When it comes to valuations and structure; they want to take on the role of an investment bank or mergers and acquisition specialist, a dealmaker. But as previously mentioned they're not trained in this. When they assume this role, they tend to hurt as opposed to help the deal. Be wary of this type of business brokers. They are more transaction facilitators. At this they are very good in facilitating the process because they have a vested interest to make the transaction happen. One business broker told me this: *at the end of the day, I just facilitate. If there is a willing buyer and a willing seller, my job is to make the transaction work and make them both happy.* I've seen brokers do exactly that and I have seen brokers that are obstacles to the deal. Just like any anything else, when a middleman is involved, depending on that individual's attitude and proactive role, the deal is going to be fluid and successful or very bumpy and possibly unsuccessful.

I like to use the business brokers that are newer. I can control the process. I've been doing this so long and I've worked with so many business brokers. I must get 10 listings a day if not more from business brokers. I've worked with hundreds of different business brokers, individuals, business broker agents and companies. I know how they think. I know what they look for. New brokers tend to have less experience and they welcome someone that has experience. They're learning from me. independent of that, I get to control the process which is ultimately my endgame. If I'm going to work with the business broker, I prefer a rookie to someone that has been doing it for many years because I get to guide the process. I use it to my advantage so that we can get a win-win deal. With the more seasoned brokers, they're set in their ways. They think that they are dealmakers and mergers and acquisition experts and sometimes that train of thought gets in the way of the deal.

In conclusion, you need to have all the sourcing strategies I mentioned active at any one time. You have to have parallel strategies every day. If I have not hammered the point home enough yet, remember that at the end of the day, buying a business and getting the right business is a numbers game. The more sourcing you have, the higher the probability that you find the business you want given your deal specifications and the deal structure and valuation that you want as well. You're buying a business with little or no money of your own down in the industry, in the sphere, in this space, with the type of infrastructure that you ideally would like. Every day, you should be implementing all these different sourcing strategies and have a plan of action. That is what sets apart the ones that actually make the deals happen from the ones that keep take forever to find the perfect deal.

Chapter 9
Meeting the Seller

When meeting the Seller, I like to do what I call a three step meeting strategy with the owner. If done properly it is very effective.

Three Meeting Strategy

Initial Contact

The initial contact with the seller is the first meeting. In the direct approach methodology, you would be knocking on as many doors as you can via phone, through e-mail, through direct mail, through social media, through your network, ultimately, to speak directly to the owner. The purpose is to make sure the owner is open to entertaining the prospect of selling his business. In his mind, he will probably be excited about it. But he's not going to make that apparent. He's probably going to play hardball. He's probably going to tell you that he'll only do it for the right price. He'll tell you that he's not thinking of a selling. He'll tell you a lot of things because that's just human nature. However, at this point, in this initial first contact, you are not going any further then assuring the owner is open to this prospect. You do not want to go into any substantive conversation (this will be covered in subsequent meetings). You really just want to get a commitment to explore the possibility in a formal meeting in the immediate future. You want to create distance between this initial contact and the subsequent meetings with the seller. Your objective in this first meeting is to plant the seed of a possibility worth contemplating.

The reason is because you want the owner to assimilate this possibility and pave a positive path and atmosphere for the upcoming meetings. After this first touch, the owner is going to talk to his friends, he's going to talk to his family. He's going to feel very good. Someone is validating his effort and is willing to pay for them. There comes a sense of great pride with that and he's going to be telling a lot of people and repeating this. What he's doing is he's reaffirming what he already has been thinking about subconsciously or in private, his exit plan. You are giving him that opportunity. By having that first initial conversation, you started the materialization of that possible exit strategy. But you have to give it time. There needs to be distance between that first initial contact and the first of two meetings where you will both go into depth of a possible transaction. What you have accomplished is opened up that possibility where he's looking at you as a potential buyer. And he is doing this with joy and affirmation. You have set up the stage where in his mind the sales process has begun. That's the important part. You planted a seed and that seed is beginning to grow. During the next two meetings, you want that seed to harvest into the culmination of a deal.

Second Meeting

In the first meeting, a second meeting has now been arranged by both you and the seller to now go into depth about a possible business transaction. This a formal meeting although it is informal in its essence. This meeting is emotional for the seller, although he will probably not show it. The most important objective in this meeting is establishing rapport with the seller. It is about positioning yourself as the best possible buyer, the most qualified buyer. You want to relay and ultimately convince the business owner the he can trust you. You want to give him the confidence and the peace of mind that the transfer of ownership is going to someone that is capable, serious and capable of continuing his legacy. This is vital. I suggest that this meeting preferably be off site and not at the business location. If it's at the business, there tends to be a level of self-consciousness from the owner. The employees are walking in and out. They may be able to hear the conversation and the owner is going to be aware of that. That's is not going to allow him to be himself, to fully open up. You want to create an ambiance where this is more of a conversation between friends as opposed to a business meeting. If the meeting is at the business, the owner may need to attend to things. He may need to take calls, look at files, talk to suppliers, talk to employees, in general, deal with day to day activities. In other words, he's going to be juggling the business and you at the same time. That's not conducive to establishing a great ambience where you are able to position yourself as the ideal buyer because you're not going to be. You will not have his undivided attention. You're not going to have 100% of his attention. You become one more business meeting of many. I highly recommend that this first meeting be off site in a neutral place where you both can deal one on one as human beings and not so much as a buyer and a seller.

Establishing rapport, creating a sense of trust an ambiance of trust and openness is critical in this meeting. If you accomplish this, and it is critical that you do, he will stop looking at you as a stranger and see you more as the person that can take over the business, can protect his legacy, can protect what he has built. He will begin to authentically open up and tell you all about his business. And you want to encourage this. Allow him to talk about the business, the history, the products and services, the employees, the hard times, the good times, his family, whatever his favorite football team, his favorite baseball team, whatever he wants to talk about. You want to encourage this and listen. You want him to open up. This is the process needed to develop a strong bond of trust at this stage so that the owner begins to convince himself that not only is a possibility of a sale in reach and it's beginning to materialize, but that it's going to the right person. The more he opens up, the more trust is being established. And this leads to the business owner believing that he is talking to his successor. That the business is going to the correct buyer. Someone that is going to take it to the next level. The future owner that is going to do everything that he couldn't or didn't want to do. That is going to preserve his legacy. That is going to protect his employees, his clients, his suppliers, his name and reputation which he has worked so hard to build.

To establish rapport, talk about your life. Talk about your family. Talk about your experiences and look for a common ground. The biggest thing about human relations is that when you find common ground, you break the ice. Talk about sporting events or common experiences or children or industry or the latest news that happened in your area. Try to find common ground. Family, sporting events, and hobbies are good icebreakers. It's the beginning of a conversation were you're establishing trust and positioning yourself as the ideal buyer. Have him tell you about the company, how he started it, when he started and how hard it was to start the company. Ask about the different milestones of the company. Let him show off, let him tell you all the good things about the company. And in doing so ask him about opportunities. Let him tell you how viable the company is. That it can grow. That there's opportunities to make a great business even better. But it's important that it comes from the owner. It will give him a sense of pride that what he's built can still grow. People love to talk about what they've done and they love to talk about what they could do. Let him tell you all about these growth strategies, these new technologies and new techniques, and new employees, and new clients and new markets that he has been planning on addressing and anything else he wants to talk about with regards to opportunities.

When you establish that trust and he talks about opportunities, ask about any challenges. But phrase it in every strategic matter such as: *It sounds like this business is doing great. Can it be doing better? Have you had any challenges preventing this? Has it been tough at any time?* Let him talk to you about his challenges. Let him talk to you about his frustrations. Let him tell you about what hinders success. What he's really doing is he's blaming other people other than himself about any problems with the company. Every company has difficulties, every company has struggles, every company has challenges. Most owners will talk at length with regards to the challenges and the struggles and how to make the business even better. They will be venting and will also give you an indication of what can and can't be fixed. So just like he talked about opportunities, him telling you about the challenges is also a means for you to see how you can add value once you become the owner. Let that happen, let it be more a one-way conversation than a two-way conversation as long as the owner wants to.

There will come a point where he's going to ask about you. He is going to want to assure himself that you are the right fit for the company he now wants to sell. So you need to be prepared for this. You need to have a good speech ready. You need to incorporate who you are as a person, your education, your professional background and how your skill sets are ideal for this company. You need to do your research prior to the meeting. Then, regurgitate a lot of the things that he's told you about opportunities and challenges and convince him on how you can address these. This is real positioning. You are convincing him, using his words, his thoughts, that you can make his company viable going forward. That you can materialize the opportunities and mitigate the challenges. That he's entrusting his business in the right hands. As you listen to him, try to identify the seller's true motives for selling: Is he frustrated? Is he tired? Does he have issues with partners? Is there lack of ideas? Are there personal problems beyond the company? Does he want to cash out? Incorporate all this and convince him that you can fill the voids. You have the potential to take it to a different level. Relay trust and prove that you are the ideal buyer for his company. Do not in any way criticize the company or point out problems. This is counter-productive to the objective.

Third Meeting

Assuming the second meeting accomplished its objective, you will request a third meeting to look at the business in person and gather specific information. The third meeting should take place in the business location. You want to tour the facility at this stage. You're going to want to meet key employees if the owner is willing to do that. Some owners will still be very reluctant at this stage to tell the employees. It's still early in the process: they don't have an offer, they don't have anything signed, you haven't given them an indication of value. They may be very reluctant to bring in any employees at this stage for fear that the employees might get nervous or feel unstable. However, if you are able to meet with employees, underscore how much the owner values them and how important they are to the business. And how important they will be to the future growth of the company. They will become your biggest cheerleaders down the line when the owner tells them he wants to sell the company. If that happens, you want the employees to go to bat for you, to root for you. It's important that you calm their fears and make them feel indispensable. Make them feel like they're integral, they've been integral in the history of the company and they're integral to the future of the company.

At this meeting, you want to clarify any doubts that you may have based on the first meeting, based on any due diligence that you did between the second meeting and third meeting, any market research that you would have done, customer reviews or any other resources you researched. This third meeting is when you want to have answers. Clarify anything you have found or that you feel needs to be addressed. Then, it is important to talk about the next step. This is when you inform him to expect an offer in the form of a letter of intent. A Letter of Intent (LOI) is the offer. But it is nonbinding. If the deal falls through, nothing happens, there's no real legal ramifications. However, there are three things that an LOI does achieve: one is you gain exclusivity. If another buyer appears, he cannot negotiate with them because he is dealing exclusively with you. The second thing it accomplishes is establishes a time frame to consummate a transaction. You want to ask for at least 60 days. This gives you ample time to do due diligence and obtain necessary financing. And the third is he allows you to do a due diligence on the business. He will allow you to analyze in detail all aspects of the business. If it has not been brought up, you're going to want to offer him a Non-Disclosure Agreement (NDA). With an NDA, you agree to keep all the information that you've received confidential for a certain period of time. You are agreeing to safeguard any information that the owner has shared with you during the previous meetings and that he will be sharing in the future. A nondisclosure agreement is binding and protects the seller. And lastly you need to make it very clear that you will request specific information to make him an offer. He will need to facilitate this information which will be protected by the NDA. You're going to want to leave this meeting with this expectation.

Information Requirements

Now that we have met with the owner in three different occasions and have agreed to move forward, we need to send him an offer. This will be sent to the owner in the form of an LOI. There are four essential elements, that need to be defined: 1) is it an asset or an equity purchase, 2) the valuation or purchase price, 3) how is the purchase going to be financed or the structure of the purchase, and 4) what, if any will the owner's participation be. We need to have clarity on these four fronts to make an offer.

We normally ask for this information after the third meeting, although at times the trust and relationship established with the seller is good enough to ask for it shortly after that second meeting. Either way, you're going to request this information. It's important to note that it simple information in terms of the overall information you're eventually going to require from the business if you get to the due diligence stage. At this stage we just want the bare minimum information so you can ascertain if there is in fact a deal to be made. We will need to analyze their assets, sales, earnings, and liabilities to determine the value of the business as well as the financial structure, if the business can be financed 100% with its own assets, liabilities and the owner or if we will need to raise additional equity or debt. It is not, however, a time for you to thoroughly understand how to run the business. It's also not time for us to confirm or validate all the information pertaining to the business. This is due diligence material. Any information already received or the information we will request we will take as valid at this stage, subject to due diligence. I also would not recommend retaining any lawyers or accountants yet, because we still do not have a deal. We are still determining whether this is a good deal or not, if this is a business we want to move forward with or discard and move on to the next.

There are five pieces of information that you want to request from the Owner: 1) Financial Information, 2) Client Concentration, 3) Employee information, 4) the owner's participation after the purchase and 5) any specific licenses, permits or certifications required to operate the business. The first is the most important piece of information and it is obligatory to determine a valuation and a financial structure. The other four are necessary to confirm your desire to move forward with an offer or not.

Financial Statements

You want to request at least three years' worth of financial statements and any interim statements available. Three years will give you an accurate picture of how the company has been performing recently. The two main statements are the Income statement and the Balance Sheet. From the Income Statement you want to understand their sales, sales trends, sales stability, the stability of their margins, and the stability of their expenses.

You want to understand recurring and non-recurring expenses. You want to be able to determine any trends here and see if this is a stable or cyclical business. You also want to look at the owner's benefit and understand any addbacks. You want to determine if these are sensible addbacks or business expenses that don't qualify as addbacks. You want to ultimately arrive at a comfort level with regards to sales, expenses and the earnings of the company.

The balance sheet is where you're going to verify what type of assets and liabilities the business has. We want to have a clear understanding of the inventory, accounts receivable, cash on hand, equipment, machinery, real estate and any other physical asset that may be used for asset based financing. These are the assets we will be using to finance the purchase. We also need to understand the liabilities. We want to understand any accounts payable, any short term loans and any long term debt. Determine if the debt is specific to the business or if it is personally guaranteed by the owner. We need to determine what debt can be assumed and what debt will need to be paid off. Part of financing the purchase is for the existing debt to remain in the business and thus reduce the purchase price by an equal amount.

Client Concentration

We want to understand the client base and customer concentration. It is imperative to understand if sales are concentrated with one, two or three clients or if the client base is well diversified. The reason being is that if there is client concentration, you're going to need to determine whether that is a deal breaker or not. If sales are not diversified enough and if one of or two of those big clients were to leave, then the business would be significantly negatively impaired. We need to determine if this is a risk worth taking.

Employees

We want to understand the employee base, particularly if there are any key employees. Determine if there is low or high turnover rates and the tenure of the employees. If there are key employees you need to understand their tenure, their desire to stay after a business purchase, and if they can be substituted in the event they leave. If there is high turnover this can be a result of the industry or a toxic business culture. We will inherit this and must be able to address it. Also, understanding the employee base will be key to determine the owner's involvement after the purchase.

Owner Involvement

We need to determine what the owner's involvement will be after the purchase, if any. There will be a natural period of transition that can range from 30 to 90 days as part of the purchase of the business. This is to assure a smooth transition of ownership and training of the new owner. However, will we be employing the owner as an employee or consultant? This is a common practice in small businesses purchases. Many business owners want to participate in the business after they sale it. They still have allegiance and loyalty to their clients, to their suppliers, to their employees and to their community. This could be beneficial for us if we want to work ON the business as he may assist in the day to day operations while we concentrate on the strategic growth of the company. But this can prove to be conflicting if we want to work IN the business as we may be butting heads more time then not and creating an environment of confusing for the employees, clients and suppliers.

Licenses, Permits or Certifications

Lastly, we need to understand if there are any specific licenses, certifications or other permits that we will need to operate the business. For instance, if we're buying a restaurant or a bar we're going to need a liquor license or a beer and wine license. If we're buying a pest control company, we're going to need a pest control license that is given out by the state. If we're buying an accounting company we're going to need a certified public accountant who can sign tax returns and financial accounting books. We want to make sure that there are employees that fulfil some of these requirements or that we have temporary agreement in place to continue using the license, permit or certification of the owner while we obtain ours.

This is the minimal information we're going to require from the owner. This will help us value the company, see if there is a viable financing structure, understand if we will need financing from the Seller, determine the seller's role post purchase, and be able to operate seamlessly after transfer of ownership with the necessary safeguards in place with regards to licenses, permits or certifications required by law.

Seller Remorse

Business owners have heard of buyer's remorse but may not be familiar with a similar term, "seller's remorse". It is likely, however, they have had conversations with friends who after selling their company experienced seller's remorse without knowing that it had a name. What exactly is this? Is it even real?

The Merriam-Webster Dictionary defines it as "a feeling of being sorry for doing something bad or wrong in the past: a feeling of guilt." Most owners would not apply that definition to how they anticipate feeling when they sell their company. In fact, euphoria, exhilaration, and relief are probably closer to what they expect to be feeling, certainly not remorse. What could they possibly be sorry for, feel guilty about, or regret? After all, this is the day they have long been waiting for, anticipating the way life will be once they have sold their company and moved on. And while seller remorse is associated with post-closing, it can occur during the sales process and derail a possible sale. Seller remorse is certainly something a buyer needs to be conscious of during the entire process.

Owners have definitely heard the horror stories from friends about all the things they thought would happen with their sale and did not or, worse, all the things they never thought would happen and did. Just look at some common disappointments:

1. I thought I would get a better price after all my years of hard work.
2. I had no idea I would pay so much in taxes and fees and net so little.
3. I thought they would keep my key employees.
4. I never thought they would move the business.
5. I thought they would keep me on longer as a consultant; I wanted to stay involved.
6. I am not enjoying retirement as much as I thought I would…I waited so long.
7. I thought I would have enough money to live the life I wanted...but I don't.
8. I never thought I would miss going to the office… but I do.

9. I never thought they would radically change the company...but they did.
10. I never knew I had other sale or transition options.

This list looks like a lot more like disappointments, disillusionment, and dissatisfaction than remorse. But these can lead to feelings of remorse, triggered by self-blame and guilt. An owner may feel ultimately responsible when the sale has negatively impacted the family, the employees, or the community. The former owner feels he or she should have known more, been better prepared, and been able to better control the outcomes. Unfortunately, the owner rarely gets a second chance. The sale of a business is not a dress rehearsal; you usually get one opportunity in a lifetime.

The primary Reasons for Seller Remorse Are:

Still Having Passion for Their Business

It's human nature to want to continue doing what you enjoy. A red flag goes up when I hear a potential seller say he or she still has a passion for the business. It raises the question of whether the potential seller is seriously committed to letting go of the business. While passion is an essential element to building a successful business, it may interfere with a seller achieving the important personal and financial goals the sale of a business would accomplish.

Perceived Loss of Identity and Self-Worth

Many owners' key relationships have been developed as a result of running their company and their self-worth is often largely based on being recognized in the community as the owner of a successful company.

Concern Regarding Leaving Money on the Table

This is a frequent concern, especially to owners trying to sell the business themselves or who have been approached by one buyer. The last thing they want do is to repeatedly wonder or wake up in the middle of the night thinking that they could have sold their business for a significantly higher valuation.

Worry About What to Do with Their Life After Selling

This can be a significant issue. There is more pain associated with the fear of the unknown (life after selling) than with the known - continuing to run the business with its structure and schedule and how it presently impacts your life. Human nature will typically avoid the pain of the unknown. This is a major reason why acquisition transactions fall apart before closing or avoided until no other sale alternative is available.

Remember, sellers will almost always go through it and it's a very normal reaction by them. They have usually invested a ton of time and sweat into running their business. They have an emotional attachment to it. Selling the company means the end of a chapter in their life; it's a new routine for them. They have built friendships along the way. They have relationships with customers, suppliers, landlords and other local businesses. Then, after the sale, it will all be gone.

It's certainly understandable that they can go through some mixed emotions. It's unlikely that they will back out of any deal because of it, but they need their time to process and digest what's happening. And so, if you find yourself in a similar situation, the response isn't to push back with any abrupt positioning.

Instead, it's the time for you to hold back any commentary. It's best to simply tell the seller, "I appreciate what you are going through. This is a big change for you. I also know you want to exit the business, so if you want to take a step back for a few days from the process then no problem. All I ask is that if you decide not to go through with our deal, please let me know immediately so I can move on to something else." By taking this approach you're allowing them to take a breather while at the same time letting them know that the deal does hang in the balance. Ultimately, they will almost always compose themselves and get back on track quickly. After all, if they truly want to sell, they don't want to lose a qualified buyer.

If you take a logical and empathetic approach to this situation, it will in fact augment the credibility you have built up with them and they will likely appreciate it. Give them a bit of time and space and let them come to grips with the deal, so both sides can move on with getting it closed.

Chapter 10

Valuing a Business

Valuing a business is where a lot of people get stuck. This is a big mystery for many people. How much is a business worth? How do we value one? In reality, valuing a business is easy and straightforward. A business legally is an independent entity. As such it is an ongoing concern. Ongoing concern means that it's “alive” and operating independent of its owners. In the case of small businesses, what we're valuing is the value of the small business as an independent ongoing concern, a “live” entity. Everything that's going to be bought in the small business; whether it's in an asset or an equity purchase, intrinsically forms part of the value of the business. Valuation really comes down to one thing; what a willing buyer is willing to pay and what a willing seller is willing to accept. That is the actual value of anything. Even with the most sophisticated business models, if a buyer determines a business value is $500,000 and the seller values it at $750,000, no matter how much empirical evidence we show either one, neither one may budge and thus the valuation on paper is worthless. It doesn't really matter what the empirical evidence or the formulas sate, there is not going to be a transaction. Hence, there is no value for that business because there wasn't a willing buyer and a willing seller that came together to determine a value for the business.

There are over 100 valuations scenarios to value businesses, assets, among many other things that are directly or indirectly related to a business. I will introduce the three internationally approved methods for business valuations, and by far the most widely used. These are the income based approach, the market based approach and the asset based approach. These three approaches are used by the BIG 4 accounting firms, Deloitte, Ernst & Young, PriceWaterhouseCoopers and KPMG. These are also promulgated by the American Society of Appraisers, which is internationally renowned for valuation methodology. These three business methodologies are used by the Small Business Administration (SBA) in the United States. If we do obtain an SBA loan, they will use these three methodology so it's important that we are familiar with them at least.

The Income Based Approach

The income approach method has 3 primary premises or assumptions. The first premise relates to the relationship between risk and reward. Depending on the level of risk, the reward should be commensurate or compensated appropriately. The higher the risk, the higher the reward. The second premise is that the assets and liabilities, the capital structure of a business will have expected future returns. And that there is an expected risk inherent in these future cash returns. The third premise is the Net Present Value (NPV) hypothesis. NPV in its simplest form means that a dollar today is worth more than a dollar tomorrow because of inflation and investment. Inflation erodes the purchasing power because over time goods and services are more expensive. With investment, a dollar invested today should be worth more in the future.

The Income Approach has two methodologies: 1) The Discounted Cash Flow Method and the 2) Capitalization of Cash Flow Method.

The Discounted Cash Flow Method (DCF)

The Discounted Earnings Method of valuing a closely held business uses the following steps:

- Determine the estimated future earnings of the business
- A terminal or residual value is often determined
- The discount rate incorporates the future risk and reward and capital structure

The DCF requires projected earnings. For this, we have to make financial projections, usually for 3, 5, 7 or even 10 years, depending on our comfort level. We will use 5 year projections going forward. To create financial protections, we give sales and implied growth rates based on managerial expertise, based on industry standards or really based on any criteria we feel comfortable will reflect the future growth. We do the same for all margins, gross, operating and net. Or we can specify future expenses specifically to arrive at these margins. Really it is whatever methods best reflects the future of the company and your comfort level. These projected incomes and expenses will lead us to the projected earnings and ultimately cash flow. From these projected sales we subtract the cost of goods sold to arrive at our gross income or gross margin. Then we subtract all the indirect or fixed expenses to arrive at EBITDA, which is defined as Earnings before Interest, Taxes, Depreciation and Amortization. We then subtract depreciation and amortization to arrive at EBIT, defined as Earnings Before Interest and Taxes. Lastly, we subtract interest and taxes and we arrive at net income. This is the future net earnings of the company.

XYZ Co.					
	← Forecasts →				
P&L Data	**2018**	**2019**	**2020**	**2021**	**2022**
Sales	2,295,632	2,418,214	2,554,532	2,638,020	2,727,231
COGS	(1,046,670)	(1,092,227)	(1,149,547)	(1,178,756)	(1,206,234)
Gross profit	**1,248,962**	**1,325,987**	**1,404,985**	**1,459,264**	**1,520,997**
Operating expenses					
Sales expenses	(70,369)	(73,746)	(78,136)	(82,141)	(86,917)
Administrative expenses	(697,780)	(728,151)	(746,365)	(773,171)	(804,156)
	(768,149)	(801,898)	(824,501)	(855,311)	(891,073)
EBITDA:	480,813	524,090	580,484	603,953	629,924
Depreciation	(48,081)	(52,409)	(58,048)	(60,395)	(62,992)
Amortization	0	0	0	0	0
EBIT (Operating profit)	432,731	471,681	522,436	543,558	566,932
Interest	(16,782)	(18,321)	(21,345)	(23,212)	(25,184)
EBT	415,949	453,360	501,091	520,346	541,748
Tax Rate	20.0%	25.0%	30.0%	35.0%	20.0%
Taxes	(83,190)	(113,340)	(150,327)	(182,121)	(108,350)
Net Earnings/ Net Income	349,541	358,341	372,108	361,437	458,582

We then need to convert these projected earnings to expected free cash flows. To do this, we add back and depreciation or amortization as these are not cash flow expenses, rather accounting cost allotments. Then we add or subtract any changes in working capital or working capital needs in the future. If our Accounts Receivables and/or our inventory increased, then they are using cash. However, if our accounts payable increase then that is a source of cash, or cash that is not being used. The net effect of these movements is the change in working capital. Lastly, we subtract any capital expenditures that we may expend because they will require cash. The reason why we're subtracting capital expenditures is because they're necessary to create those specific future earnings. These result in Free Cash Flows (FCF) per projected year.

Net Earnings/ Net Income	349,541	358,341	372,108	361,437	458,582
Plus depreciation and amortization	48,081	52,409	58,048	60,395	62,992
Cash flow	397,623	410,750	430,157	421,832	521,575
-Investment in working capital	15,501	(14,724)	(16,373)	(10,028)	(10,715)
-Capex	(91,825)	(96,729)	(102,181)	(105,521)	(109,089)
Free cash flow (FCF)	321,299	299,298	311,602	306,283	401,770

We also need to determine a terminal value. A terminal value is used because one cannot project into infinity. And the underlying assumption is that the business will survive for a very long time, far longer than the projections made. It assumes that the business is going to be an ongoing concern indefinitely. Terminal value captures these future earnings beyond the projections. The terminal value assumes that growth after the projection period is now normalized. The "normalized" level of cash flow anticipated in the period immediately following the end of the discrete projection period, and for all following periods, is converted to a "terminal value," typically through a capitalization/value multiple process. The terminal value is determined by the formula of multiplying the FCF of year 5 by the growth rate and dividing this by the value of the discount rate minus the normalized growth rate. This will give us the terminal value at year five.

Now we need to bring all these FCFs future cash flows in our projections including the terminal value to their present value. We do this using a discount rate explained below. First we take all the projected FCFs and discount them to the present value. Then we take the terminal value and discount that to the present value. Then we sum these 2 cash flow numbers together to arrive at the Net Present Value of all the FCFs. This gives us the Enterprise Value (EV) of the company.

However, we ultimately want to obtain the Equity value of the company which is the value of the shareholders or owners of the company. The Equity value by definition is the EV less any interest bearing debt plus any cash (cash is always stated at its NPV by definition). So the last step in the DCF method is to subtract any interest bearing debt and add any cash on hand. This gives the Equity Value of the business or the Value of business to the owners.

	←Forecasts→				
	2018	2019	2020	2021	2022
Free cash flow (FCF)	**321,299**	**299,298**	**311,602**	**306,283**	**401,770**
Variation in FCF		*-7%*	*4%*	*-2%*	*31%*
Discount rate (WACC)	**17.5%**				
Discounted FCF	273,383	216,685	191,950	160,537	179,181
Present Value of Projected Cash Flows FCFs	1,021,737				
Present value of Terminal Value FCF	1,270,450				
Enterprise Value	**2,292,187**				
Less debt	(693,121)				
Plus Cash	70,149				
Equity Value 100%	**1,669,215**				

The discount rate that is used to bring all the aforementioned future cash flows is based on the business's Cost of Capital. This is determined by the business's Capital Structure. Money (capital) needed to run a company comes from either borrowing (debt) or the owners' money (equity). The cost of capital is either the interest payment on the debt or the required profit that the owners want in return for their investment, the "expected return". When you have a capital structure that combines both the interest rate of debt and the 'expected return' of the investors/owners, we arrive at the total cost of capital. If the cost of debt (e.g. interest) and cost of equity (expected return) are different, which is almost always the case, then we have to get an average of the two to get our cost of capital. Cost of capital is expressed as a percentage; because it's compared to the total capital (as a percentage of the total capital). What if your company has more debt vs. equity, or vice versa? The formula must give more importance or weight to whichever is bigger; and must give lesser weight to whichever is smaller. Thus, we have the WACC or Weighted Average Cost of Capital concept. This is the basic WACC or Weighted Average Cost of Capital Formula: WACC = (Debt Proportion) (Cost of Debt %) (1 - tax rate %) + (Equity Proportion) (Cost of Equity %). The WACC is ultimately the discount rate used to bring all these future cash flows to the present value (WACC is explained in detail in a section below).

The Capitalization Cash Flow Method (CCF)

The second method in the income based approach is the capitalization of cash flow method. This method is often applied to established businesses with stable earnings. It is assumed that the business is more mature and thus will have expected normalized future earnings. Whereas, the DCF is used with business that have different growth rates and different margin rates. Here we're talking about a normalized growth rate and normalized margins so the variations from year to year should be very minimal if any.

The steps are very similar to the DCF method in terms of estimated free cash flow, your cost of capital (WACC), and then arriving at EV and ultimately the Equity value. The general steps are to develop a "normalized" level of expected earnings. Then convert these normalized earnings to expected cash flow. Then calculate the cost of capital or WACC. And then we convert the WACC to a direct capitalization rate. To do this, you subtract the expected normalized growth rate form the WACC (WACC-Growth Rate). Then we "capitalize" the expected cash flow by dividing it by the capitalization rate. Capitalization Rate = (WACC –g) and the Capitalization Multiple = 1/(WACC –g). Subsequently we subtract interest-bearing debt and add any cash to arrive at the Equity value.

Equity Value 100%	1,669,215
CCF Valuation Analysis	
Normalized Long Term FCF	328,617
Discount rate (WACC)	17.5%
Long term growth rate	3.0%
Capitalization Rate	14.5%
Enterprise Value	2,262,132
Less debt	(693,121)
Plus Cash	70,149
Equity Value 100%	**1,639,161**

Market Valuation Approach

The second widely accepted approach is called the market based approach to valuation. The premise behind this approach is that one arrives at a valuation based on the pricing multiples observed for similar businesses that were sold or publicly traded companies that are being traded on the public stock exchanges. There are two methods within the market approach, 1) the guideline transaction method and 2) the guideline public company method.

The Guideline Transaction Method

The Guideline Transaction Method values a business based on pricing multiples derived from the sale of companies that are similar to the company we want to buy.

The primary steps in the Guideline Transaction Method include:

1. Finding transactions involving the purchase of comparable companies
2. Selecting the transactions that closely mirror the company's operations and which occurred in similar industry and economic conditions

3. Applying the indicated pricing multiples from the representative transactions

Valuation experts typically subscribe to databases that allow them to perform searches for comparable transactions. For our purposes, we can obtain the data from business brokers and online. The companies involved in the guideline transactions typically differ from the target company in their respective stages of development and size, but they should have comparable operational characteristics and financial risks. The comparable transactions also reflect the economic conditions of the industries in which the target company operates of similar size, companies with similar margins, and transactions that have occurred most recently. Thus, the comparative analysis to the target company being valued is based on the performance and characteristics of the sample as a whole rather than on any individual transaction selected.

It should be noted that the calculated transaction multiples are typically based on the enterprise value of the purchased companies, meaning that we arrive at an enterprise value of the target company when using the Guideline Transaction Method. Enterprise value incorporates all of a company's operating assets, except for cash, and includes working capital, fixed assets and intangible assets. Because enterprise value indicates the value of a company's equity and interest-bearing debt (excluding cash), one must subtract debt and add cash to the calculated enterprise value to arrive at the company's equity value. Below is an Example of the Transactions:

Year	Purchaser	Target	Country (target)	Transcati (US$ M)	% acquisition	EV multiples	
						Sales	EBITDA
2016	Valeo SA	Johnson Controls Automotive Electronics	USA	174	100%	0.3	3.4
2017	Absolute Ventures	RACO SpA	IT	39	100%	0.7	4.5
2017	BorgWarner Inc	Beru AG	GE	440	62%	1.4	3.5
2017	Absolute Ventures	Momo Aftermarket	IT	27	100%	0.9	5
2016	TT Electronics Plc	Optek Technology Inc	USA	30	100%	0.8	4.5
2017	Hg Capital	WET Automotive AG	GE	154	66%	1.2	5.2
2017	Dura Automotive Systems Inc	Heywood Williams Group	UK	100	100%	0.4	4.9
2017	Tomkins Plc	Stackpole Ltd	CAN	189	52%	0.3	4.9
				Min		0.30	3.40
				Max		1.40	5.20
Average						0.75	4.5

The Guideline Public Company Method

The Guideline Public Company Method values a business based on trading multiples derived from publicly traded companies that are similar to the target company.

The steps in applying the Guideline Public Company Method include:

1. Identifying comparable public companies
2. Adjusting the guideline public company multiples for differences in the size and risk of these companies compared to the target company
3. Applying the adjusted pricing multiples from the representative companies

Ideally, the guideline public companies selected for analysis compete in the same industry as the target company. When such publicly-traded companies do not exist (or when only a small number of them exist), other companies with similar underlying characteristics such as markets serviced, growth, risks or other relevant factors can be considered – exact comparability is not required under this method of valuation, although a closer comparable is preferred.

As mentioned above, the guideline public company multiples may be adjusted for differences in the size and risk of the guideline companies compared to the target company being valued. Typically, this results in a downward adjustment to the guideline public company multiples.

Similar to the Guideline Transaction Method, the guideline public companies differ from the target company in their respective stages of development and size, but they have comparable operational models and financial risks. They also reflect the economic conditions of the industries in which the target company operates. Thus, the comparative analysis to the target company being valued is based on the performance and characteristics of the sample as a whole rather than on any individual guideline company selected.

Also similar to the Guideline Transaction Method, the calculated multiples are often based on the enterprise values of the guideline public companies, meaning that we arrive at an enterprise value of the target company when using the Guideline Public Company Method. Therefore, one must subtract debt and add cash to the calculated enterprise value to arrive at the company's equity value. Below is an Example of the Public Companies:

Company	Country	EV/Sales	P/BV	EV/EBITDA	Market Cap (US$M)	Sales (US$M)	Debt (US$M)	Cash (US$M)
Beru AG	GE	2.1	2.5	7.1	1,041	493	24	54
Dura Automotive Systems	USA	0.5	0.1	6.4	42	2,344	1,143	102
Faurecia	FR	0.3	0.6	4.4	1,820	13,318	2,472	533
Magna International I	CAN	0.4	1.3	3.4	9,590	22,811	920	1,682
Sanluis Corporación	MX	0.6	1.2	7.1	122	628	292	29
Sogefi	IT	0.8	2.7	6.4	755	1,272	265	65
Valeo SA	FR	0.4	1.3	6.4	3,601	11,545	2,551	1,153
Visteon Corp	USA	0.1	N.A.	7.2	591	16,976	1,994	865
Average		0.45	1.3	6.1				

To summarize, the guideline public company method is a market based approach to valuation that is based on the pricing multiples derived from comparable public companies whereas the guidelines transaction method is a market based approach to valuation based on the pricing multiples derived from comparable transactions of sold companies.

So let's put it all together through an example. We will use 2018 Estimated EBITDA as our earnings, $480,813. We will apply the 4.5 average multiple from the Guideline Transaction Method and the 6.1 average multiple from the Guideline Public Company Method and arrive at an Enterprise Value range of $1.861,638 and $2,908,916. From this range we subtract the debt to arrive at an Equity Value range of $1,168,517 and $2,215,795. The midpoint to this would give us an implied Equity Value of $1,692,156.

Price Multiple Valuation Approach		
XYC Co. data		
Equity (Dec. 31, 2017)	318,623	
Net debt (Dec. 31, 2017)	693,121	
Sales 2017	2,214,523	
Sales 2018E	2,295,632	
EBITDA 2017	414,850	
EBITDA 2018E	480,813	
Multiples to be considered		
	Range	
EV/EBITDA	4.49	6.05
Enterprise Value Range	1,861,638	2,908,916
Less Debt	(693,121)	(693,121)
Equit Value	1,168,517	2,215,795

Asset Based Valuation Approach

The third approach is the asset-based approach. This approach values the business based on the market value, the replacement costs and or the liquidation value of the assets and liabilities. The asset based method uses the cost approach on your balance sheet of all your assets as the starting point of value.

There are three methods in the asset approach; you have the adjusted net book value method, the liquidation value method, and the replacement value method. The most widely used method out of the three is the adjusted net book value method. GAAP accounting requires that all assets are recorded at historical cost minus an appropriate accumulated depreciation or impairments or amortization. This is not reflective of the actual true value of the assets. For instance, GAAP requires plant and equipment ("fixed assets") to be carried on the books at original cost and depreciated over allowable recovery periods which, as a rule, is shorter than the assets' actual productive life. This difference results in a rapid "write-off" of assets. Frequently, investments in equipment are virtually eliminated from the balance sheet, although the assets themselves are still utilized in operations. (The same is true of buildings and improvements, which are likely to appreciate rather than depreciate in value.). Because of these accounting practices, depreciated book values generally understate the true value of fixed assets.

Similarly, most long term liabilities are recording at the time the liabilities were contracted. Under GAAP, these rates are not adjusted to reflect any market changes. In a publicly traded company, if interest rates go up or down the value of their debt would also go up and down but that's not being reflected in their balance sheet.

And finally GAAP general accepted accounting principles does not permit the recognition of numerous and frequently valuable assets such as trademarks, trade names, logos, goodwill that are not on the balance sheet as well as liabilities such as long term leases, contingent litigation, and other contingencies so you have to account for these as well.

The Net Adjusted Book Value Method

The net adjusted book value method takes the values represented on the balance sheet and brings those assets and liabilities to current market values. The adjusted net-assets basis, seeks to address the problem of the (accounting) book value of certain assets (as shown on the balance sheet) bearing no relation to their actual market value. This method disregards their original cost or what the depreciation has been and brings the assets to market value. It also takes any off balance sheet assets and liabilities and adds those to the assets and liabilities on the balance sheet. It then takes the net asset value of all the assets including the off balance sheet assets and subtracts them from the market value of the liabilities to arrive at the net asset value of the company. It's very straightforward. Below is an example:

BALANCE SHEET December 31, 2017			
	Historical	Normalized Adjustments	Net Adjusted Book Value
Current Assets			
Cash	70,149	-	70,149
Accounts Reivables	278,235	-	278,235
Inventories	487,523	-	487,523
Prepaid expenses	12,531	-	12,531
		-	-
Total Current Assets	848,438	-	848,438
Fixed Assets			
Machinery and Equipment	623,123	123,214	746,337
Transportation Equipment	78,456	(10,236)	68,220
Office Equipment	45,321	(9,365)	35,956
Computer Equipment	14,231	(3,521)	10,710
Accumulative Depreciation	(194,531)	194,531	-
Total Fixed Assets:	566,600	294,623	861,223
Total Assets	1,415,038	294,623	1,709,661
Current Liabilities			
Accounts Payable	374,523	-	374,523
Income taxes payable	14,536	-	14,536
Deffered Expenses	14,235	-	14,235
Total Current Liabilities:	403,294	-	403,294
Bank Loan	693,121	-	693,121
Total Long Term Liabilities	693,121	-	693,121
Total Liabilities:	1,096,415	-	1,096,415
Shareholder's Equity			
Paid In Capital	118,452	294,623	413,075
Accumulated Retained Earnings	200,171	-	200,171
Total Shareholder's Equity	318,623	294,623	613,246

The Liquidation Value Method

The liquidation value method is preferably used for businesses that are going out of business or are in distress. It's a methodology that represents the book value of the business based on its liquidation values, its disposable values. This method of valuation does not consider the business as an on-going company. It assumes that the business will cease operating, sell its assets and pay its liabilities. Any leftover cash would go to the owners. This calculation is only meaningful in establishing an absolute bottom price below which an owner would be better off to liquidate the company than to sell. The liquidation value takes into account the fact that the assets -- inventory, property, and equipment -- would not bring in as much if they were sold "under pressure" as they would if the company were to continue in business. Some general rules of thumb for liquidation values are:

- 80% of all accounts receivable less than 90 days old.
- 50% of all inventory.
- 40% of the current market value of equipment.
- 25% of the current market value of buildings.
- 40% of the current market value of land.
- 0% for leasehold improvements.

The Replacement Value Method

The third one is the replacement value method which is the method that takes the book value of the business assets and liability based on what it will take for one to replace these assets and or these liabilities. This value is the current market cost of reproducing the fixed assets of the business (property, fixtures, leasehold improvements, equipment). In all instances, it accounts for off balance sheet assets as well as liabilities, so it's very straightforward.

Valuing a Small Businesses

Even though we can use the 3 Valuation approaches previously discussed, ultimately we use the Market Approach as the most widely used. For this, we use a multiple of earnings, be it EBITDA, EBIT or owners benefit.

One word of caution, before we get into valuation, let's understand owners benefit also known as Seller's Discretionary Cash Flow (SDC) a bit more. As previously mentioned, what a lot of brokers have told and convinced sellers is that they can start adding certain expenses back to the net income that were originally subtracted from the revenue. Many of these expenses are the owner's personal expenses and compensation that pass through the income statement. So owner's benefit by definition is net income plus all these add backs as they are called. However, some are real business operating expenses. I have a high degree of scrutiny when I look at these type of financial statements because they become subjective. Regular and none regular operating business expenses are added back. Now, there's two sides to this coin. There's obvious add backs such as owner compensation, health benefits if other employees are getting them, and a computer. But if we needed to replace someone to cover the responsibilities of the owner, then why would I add back the owner's compensation? We are going to have that expense anyways. If there's travel involved for business purposes and they're adding that back, we're still going to have to travel and go to those same trade shows and conferences and sales visits. So why would this be added back as a benefit? Expenses like these, I highly scrutinize. Sometimes a seller adds back the salary of a family member. The same logic must be applied; if we have to replace a family member, then I have to incur that expense anyway. These are black and white business expenses that should not be added back.

Many sellers or business owners want to minimize their tax burden. They may add their groceries, their mortgage payment, or their home utilities and treat them all as a business expense. These are expenses that are personal and not business related. They're passing through the business so that they lower their fiscal exposure and pay less taxes. Those I allow. But then you have some in between, ones which are not so readily identifiable as a business or personal expense. Examples would be cellular expenses or gasoline or automobile expenses or certain travel. Businesses may or may not pay for those expenses. It's a gray area and really at the owner's discretion. As an outsider, these and others may be hard to detect. We need to be very cautious and highly scrutinize all add backs. Make sure you receive clear and definable explanations for these.

What is commonly used in the industry is EBITDA or EBIT if there is not much depreciation or amortization. This is the earnings that I like to use to value a small company and not owner's benefit. As a rule of thumb, we usually apply a multiple of 3-5 times earnings. So if a business has an EBITDA of $250,000, then the business would be valued in the $750,000 to $1,250,000 range. If you decide to use owner's benefit, as a rule of thumb, you apply a 2 to 4 times multiple. Now, the question would be, why three and not five or why not four? Essentially, what is the precise multiple to use? This is where valuation for small businesses becomes more of an art than a science. There is no direct response, there is no direct correlation. Ideally, we would find comparable sales that will ultimately give us the average multiple. But it really comes down to experience. I generally know that for a restaurant, for instance, which has a higher risk then other industries, I would apply a lower multiple. Now, there's exceptions to this. But I know that from analyzing many different restaurants and buying restaurants that I could get away with a 3 times multiple of EBITDA or closer to the 2 times multiple of owner's benefit.

The business size is usually associated with greater strength and will coincide generally with a higher multiple. One is willing to pay more and thus use a higher multiple for a company that has earnings of $2.5 million than one that has $500,000. It may imply a broader management team, access to more financing options, larger infrastructure, more established clientele, more longevity (the business has been around for a long time), it's a market niche or a strong market presence. Think about it this way: growing a business from $500,000 to $2.5 million in earnings doesn't happen overnight. There is a natural build up and value creation process which in turn is reflected in seasoned management, seasoned processes, longer term clients, longer term supplier relationships among other things. A smaller business does not have these variables as institutionalized or as seasoned and thus commands a smaller multiple. Or maybe the growth potential is not there. Think about a *Subway* franchise. While a stable brand, it is very difficult to suddenly quadruple in size. It doesn't have growth potential. It doesn't have scalability. Even at its best performance, it has reached its limit. So, it's going to command a smaller multiple to a business that has more earning opportunities.

If you have readily available comparable transactions, that's going to be an indicator of what multiple to use. Other aspects come into play that will influence the multiple to use. Is there owner financing involved? Maybe you compensate the seller with a higher price, hence a higher multiple, to obtain owner finance and a better structure in general. It's a win-win scenario. Factors such as how institutionalized the company is. Is there a key man? If you lose a key employee; will that negatively affect the value of the company? Does it have a unique technology?

Does it have certain patents and trademarks that protect it from other competitors? Is it in a specialized niche that is not crowded? All of these things and many others need to be taken into consideration. Nonetheless, the rule of thumb is to use multiples within that 3 to 5 range for EBITDA or 2 to 4 range for owner's benefit. That is how we would go about valuing a small business. One can obtain general industry and sub industry multiples from various data source such as business brokers, the internet and specifically www.bizminer.com.

The Weighted Average Cost of Capital

The Weighted Average Cost of Capital or WACC is the discount rate used to discount future cash flows to the present value, primarily used in the Discounted Cash Flow Model. Let's explain some basic definitions. The "Cost of capital" is defined as "the opportunity cost of all capital invested in a business." Opportunity cost is what you give up as a consequence of your decision to use a scarce resource in a particular way. All capital invested is the total amount of cash invested into a business. In a business this refers to the fact that we are measuring the opportunity cost of all sources of capital which include debt and equity.

How Do We Calculate a Company's Weighted Average Cost of Capital? We calculate a company's weighted average cost of capital using a 3 step process:

1. Cost of capital components. First, we calculate or infer the cost of each kind of capital that the business uses, namely debt and equity.

   A. Debt capital. The cost of debt capital is equivalent to the company's debt, adjusted for the tax-deductibility of interest expenses. Specifically, the after-tax cost of debt-capital, long-term debt x (1 minus the marginal tax rate in %)

B. Equity capital. Equity shareholders, unlike debt holders, do not demand an explicit return on their capital. However, equity shareholders do face an implicit opportunity cost for investing in a specific company, because they could invest in an alternative company with a similar risk profile. Thus, we infer the opportunity cost of equity capital.

We can do this by using the "Capital Asset Pricing Model" (CAPM). This model says that equity shareholders demand a minimum rate of return equal to the return from a risk-free investment plus a return for bearing extra risk. This extra risk is often called the "equity risk premium", and is equivalent to the risk premium of the market as a whole times a multiplier called "beta" that measures how risky a specific security is relative to the total market. Thus, the cost of equity capital = Risk-Free Rate + (Beta times Equity Risk Premium).

2. Capital structure. Next, we calculate the proportion that debt and equity capital contribute to the entire business, using the market values of total debt and equity to reflect the investments on which those investors expect to earn a minimum return.

3. Weighting the components. Finally, we weight the cost of each kind of capital by the proportion that each contributes to the entire capital structure. This gives us the Weighted Average Cost of Capital (WACC), the average cost of each dollar of cash employed in the business.

To demonstrate how to calculate a company's cost of capital, we will use a hypothetical company, ABC Co. that operates in heavy construction as an example.

1. Cost of capital components. ABC Co. draws upon two major sources of capital from the capital markets: debt and equity.

   A. Cost of debt capital. ABC Co. had debt of $8.5 million

Our first step in calculating any company's cost of capital is to see what the cost of debt is before taxes, or the interest rate. In this case, the weighted pre-tax cost of debt would be equivalent to 11.5%. However, we are not done yet. We have to adjust for the tax-deductibility of interest expenses, which lowers the cost of debt according to the following formula:

After-Tax Cost of Debt Capital = The Yield-to-Maturity on long-term debt x (1 minus the marginal tax rate). Given ABC Co.'s marginal tax rate of 30%, the company's after-tax cost of debt equates to 11.5% x (100% minus 30%), or 8.1%.

   B. Cost of equity capital. We noted above that:

Cost of Equity Capital = Risk-Free Rate + (Beta times Market Risk Premium).

To calculate any company's cost of equity capital, we need to find a reliable source for each of these inputs:

1. Risk-free Rate. We suggest using the rate of return on long-term (ten-year) US government treasury bonds as a proxy for the risk-free rate.

2. Beta coefficient. In this case we have selected the industry beta for "Building - Heavy Construction" from the "Industry Betas "obtained from www.damodaran.com. ABC Co.'s beta is 1.66.

(There are a variety of sources available for obtaining the beta coefficient for a particular company i.e. Yahoo offers free beta estimates through its Company Profile service, Bloomberg. Free beta estimates from Bloomberg can be accessed online, and Damodaran.com for industry betas.)

3. Equity Risk Premium. Forward looking approaches, as well as more recent historical data, suggest an equity risk premium in the 3 to 5% range. Additional factors can raise this, as noted below. We use an Equity Risk Premium estimate of 7.5% for this company.

For those interested in looking at historical equity risk premium, use the following online resources: Ibbotson Associates and Aswath Damodaran.

To continue with our ABC Co. case study, we used the following estimates for these three factors: Risk-free rate of 4%, Beta coefficient of 1.66, and Equity risk premium of 7.5%.

Using these estimates, ABC Co.'s cost of equity capital = Risk-Free Rate + (Beta times Equity Risk Premium) = 4.00% + (1.66 x 7.5%), or 16.5%.

3. Weighting the components. Finally, we weight the cost of each kind of capital by the proportion that each kind of capital contributes to the entire business. This gives us the Weighted Average Cost of Capital (WACC), the average cost of each dollar of cash employed in the business.

To review, ABC Co.'s after-tax cost of debt is 8.1% and its cost of equity is 16.5%. The market value of ABC Co.'s debt is equal to $8.5 million and the market value of ABC Co.'s equity is $45 million. The value of equity can be obtained from the multiplying the # of shares outstanding by share price, 10 million shares at a per share price of $4.50 as an example.

Alternatively, for private companies, the value of the business may be computed using various valuation methods.

ABC Co.'s weighted average cost of capital is thus 8.1% x 15.9% + 16.5% x 84.1% = 15.1%. You can see this calculation in the table below:

Inputs for WACC Calculation:

Risk free rate (%)	4.00%
Yield-to-Maturity of debt (%)	11.50%
Equity risk premium (%)	7.50%
Beta of equity	1.66
Corporate tax rate (%)	30%
Common shares (MM)	10.0
Share price ($)	$ 4.50
Market value of debt ($, MM)	$ 8.5

Weighted Average Cost of Capital (WACC) Calculation

Debt	**Equity**	**Total**
Pre-tax cost of debt (%) 11.5%	Cost of equity (%) 16.5%	
Market value of debt ($, MM) $ 8.5	Market value of equity ($, MM) $ 45.0	Enterprise Value ($, MM) $ 53.5
Percent of enterprise value (%) 15.9%	Percent of enterprise value (%) 84.1%	Percent of enterprise value (%) 100.0%
Weighted Average Cost of Capital (WACC, %)		**15.1%**

Chapter 11
The Deal Structure and the LOI

Equity Vs Asset Purchase

Understanding Equity Vs Asset Purchase is the key step in determining your deal structure. As we begin to structure our deal and eventual offer to the seller, we have to determine if the purchase is the ownership interest in the business (Equity or Stock purchase) or are only selected assets being transferred without an actual transfer of the business entity (Asset purchase).

Our specific strategy involves the purchase of the Equity of the company as opposed to the purchase of the assets. The reason for this is that the legal entity that owns the business that we want to buy, is the owner of all the assets and liabilities. This includes all the inventory, accounts receivables, equipment, machinery, furniture, real estate and all the intangible assets such as goodwill, brands, trademarks, patents, image, trade secrets and the general brand of the company. It owns the cash of the business. It has a history and therefore has a credit history. It owns the client contracts and the sales and cash flow associated with it. And for this very reason, the entity is the one that will be receiving the financing for a no money down deal. All of the aforementioned assets will act as collateral for financing the purchase. It is the entity that will sign loan documents with the various financing or lending institutions and not you as the new owner.

That said, it is up to you and your comfort level if you will go forward with an Equity purchase or an Asset purchase. So, let's talk about the differences between an Equity Purchase and an Asset purchase.

Asset Purchase

In an asset purchase, the seller retains possession of the legal entity and the buyer purchases selected individual assets of the company (equipment, fixtures, licenses, goodwill, customer lists, trade names, intellectual property, and inventory). Asset sales generally do not include cash and the seller typically holds onto long-term debt obligations. Accounts receivable, prepaid expenses, accounts payable, etc. are typically included in the sale.

Buyer's Perspective

The buyer has the opportunity to select those assets which it desires while not absorbing specified liabilities. An asset sale allows buyers to "step-up" the company's depreciation. The buyer can gain tax advantages by allocating portions of the purchase price to certain asset classes to maximize annual depreciation, stabilizing cash flow in the first few critical years of the acquisition. Buyers prefer asset sales because they avoid absorbing potential liabilities (current and future), especially contingent liabilities in the form of product liability, contract disputes, warranty issues, or employee lawsuits.

Seller's Perspective

An asset purchase isn't a "clean exit" and typically involves the owner winding down the legal entity, paying off long term notes, and remaining entangled in affairs longer than they'd like. An asset sale generates a higher tax burden, lessening the actual net amount shareholders receive from sale proceeds. Intangible assets (goodwill) are taxed at capital gains rates. "Hard" assets can be subject to higher ordinary income tax rates. The legal structure of your company plays a role in determining the tax treatment. If the entity sold is a C-corporation, the seller faces double taxation. The corporation is first taxed upon selling the assets to the buyer. The corporation's shareholders are then taxed again when the proceeds transfer outside the corporation.

Equity Purchase

Through an equity purchase, the buyer purchases the selling shareholders' stock directly obtaining ownership in the seller's legal entity. Assets and liabilities not desired by the buyer will typically be distributed or paid off prior to the sale. Unlike an asset sale, stock sales do not require numerous separate conveyances of each individual asset because the ownership of each asset resides within the legal entity.

Buyer's Perspective

Buyers lose the ability to gain a stepped up basis in the assets and must utilize the book value of the asset for depreciation. This lower depreciation expense can result in a short-term reduction in cash flow and potentially higher future taxes. Buyers accept more risk by purchasing the company's stock outright. Contingencies such as lawsuits, employee suits, and other liabilities become the responsibility of the new owner.

Although the buyer typically prefers an asset sale, unassignable contracts, leases, permits, contracts, etc. held by the company may necessitate the buyer executing a stock sale. A stock sale may be a better option because the corporation, not the owner, retains ownership of the key contracts and poses little to no business interruption.

Seller's Perspective

Sellers typically favor equity purchases because all the proceeds are taxed at a lower capital gains rate (maximizing the net cash proceeds to the owner on sale). Sellers see the stock sale as a "clean break" due to their decreased responsibility/risk for future liabilities.

As previously mentioned, although we do execute on Asset purchases from time to time, we prefer to purchase a business via Equity purchase to achieve a structure whereby we do not risk our own capital and we are able to use the assets and liabilities of the target business as well as the credit history and longevity to finance the purchase.

Diagram of an Equity Sale

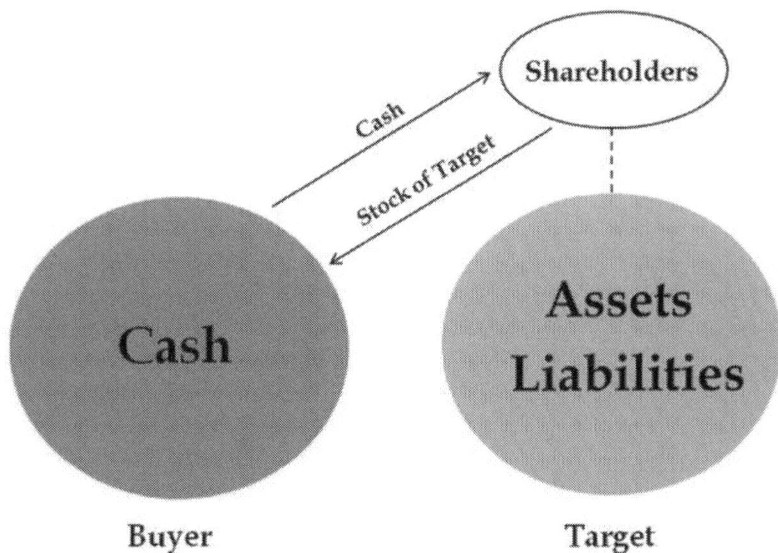

Result of an Equity Sale

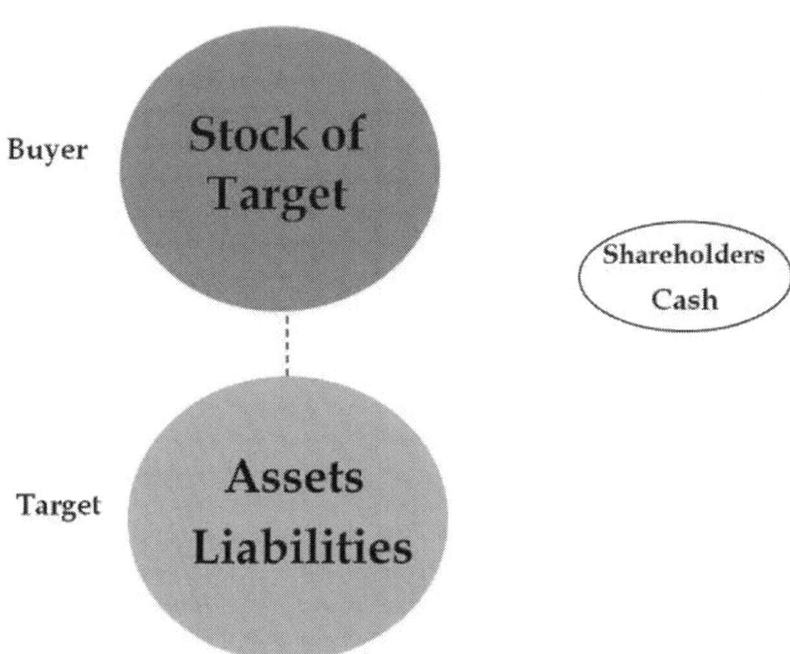

Diagram of an Asset Sale

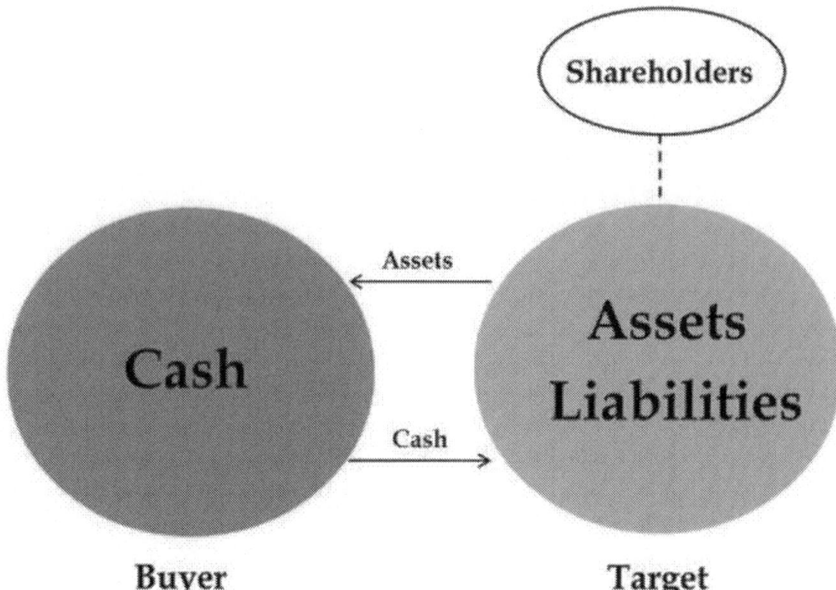

Result of an Asset Sale

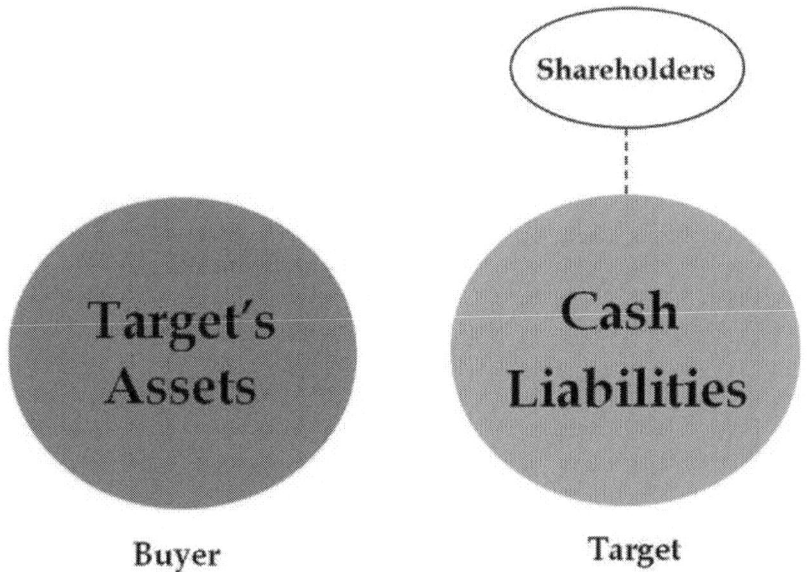

Structuring the Deal

Now that we have all the necessary financial information required, we have established a purchase price, and we are doing an Equity purchase, we need to determine how we will ultimately finance and structure the purchase. We already have a valuation; the valuation gave us a number that we have to come up with. We now have to put the financing in place with debt and owner financing. We look at the existing assets of the business and used them to finance the purchase price. We look at any existing liabilities and debt and assume those as part of the purchase price. Since we are buying the Equity of the business, all assets and liabilities are fair game for using them as a source of financing. Even the cash in the business becomes 100% source of financing as we can use it to satisfy part of the purchase price or for other cash needs as we will see below.

Asset Based Financing

The first thing we look at is the assets. In looking at the assets, we're going to concentrate on four types of assets that are readily financeable: real estate, accounts receivables, inventory and equipment. The most widely used asset is real estate. For real estate, you could get upwards to 80% of the value of the real estate, what is called the loan to value ratio. The loan to value ratio measure how much a loan will be as a percentage of the value of the asset. For instance, if an asset is worth a hundred thousand dollars, a bank may lend up to 80 thousand dollars in terms of a loan or an 80% loan to value ratio. Real estate financing can usually be paid back over a longer period of time ranging between 10 to 25 years. This asset garners a lower interest rates because it is considered one of the most secure types of collateral. Real Estate tends to go up in value. And real estate is immovable. This means that the lender know that the asset cannot be removed.

The second asset we look at is the accounts receivable. For this asset one obtains values of 80 to 90% loan to value ratios. Accounts receivable by definition are sales that have already occurred and will be collected. Essentially, a finance company will buy those receivables with recourse to the company in the event those receivables don't pay the loan. A lender will gauge the quality of the Accounts Receivables. Do the clients pay on time? Are there delinquent accounts? How often do they turnover? The better these indicators the better the quality of this asset and the higher the loan to value ratio a lending institution will finance.

The third asset class would be inventory. Inventory financing is just as it implies, taking the inventory stock and lending against it. Typically, inventory has a loan to value ratio upwards to 50%. To lenders, it is a riskier type of asset because of its mobility and ability to decay. People can take it out of the warehouse, steal it, or it can get damaged. This is why the loan to value ratio is less than the previous two asset classes mentioned. Nonetheless, it is a source of financing for a business purchase.

The fourth asset class is equipment, be it machinery, industrial equipment, trucks, technology equipment, construction, or any other type of equipment. Asset based lending on used or existing equipment has a loan to value ratio up to 50 percent. It's similar to inventory in the sense that it's movable, it could decay, which makes it a riskier asset. One can get longer terms and the interest rate isn't as expensive as receivable financing or inventory financing.

Another type of receivable financing is a merchant cash advances (MCA). Technically it is not receivable financing, it is funding your future receivables, your future sales. It is directly linked to sales and accounts receivables. Whereas receivables are sales that have already happened in the past and are on your books, merchant cash advances would be future sales. MCA is technically not based on asset financing because there is no asset on the balance sheet to lend against. Rather, they are financing future sales. The way an MCA works is by analyzing three to six months' worth of sales and their respective cash flow. They take the average of the *normalized* sales to arrive at a monthly number. They will then lend upwards of two and a half times that monthly amount. If a business is selling a hundred thousand dollars a month on average, that business can receive upwards of a $250,000 loan with merchant cash advances. They are to be repaid back in a shorter term, usually between 6, 9 months upwards to a year (although I have seen some being paid back two years). An MCA is inherently a more expensive loan. But it could provide the needed short term cash and financing for the purchase of a business.

Below is the general rule of thumb on the maximum LTV per each asset class assuming existing assets and not new assets as could be in the cases of equipment, machinery and commercial real estate.

Asset Class	Loan to Value (LTV)
Receivables	90%
Inventory	50%
Equipment	50%
Real Estate	80%
Merchant Cash Advance	2.5 X Monthly Revenue

Liability Based Financing

On the liability side, we're looking at any interest bearing debt that we can potentially assume, any short term or long term loans. They can be equipment loans, inventory loans, real estate loans, receivable loans, or even small business loans. Technically, we are not assuming anything since we are buying the legal entity and these loans have the legal entity as the debtor (if it is an Asset purchase, then we would look to assume them). However, some of these loans may have personal guarantees of the seller which will either need to be released or assumed. Other loans may have a covenant that states if there is any significant change of ownership, the lending institution needs to approve the new structure for the loan to remain in place. Accounts payable, while are technically not a debt will be subject to being assumed to finance part of the purchase price. We want to assume these loans as a way of financing the business purchase. Had it been an asset purchase, the owner would use the proceeds of the business sale to pay off all of these liabilities. In doing an Equity purchase structure and assuming these liabilities, the business purchase price will be reduced by the corresponding amount of debt "assumed". So by "assuming" or keeping existing liabilities when purchasing a business, we are in essence financing part of the purchase price.

Owner Financing

Owner financing is where the owner takes a promissory note against a portion of the purchase price. The Seller is in essence financing a part of the purchase price. Summed up another way, the seller is essentially acting as a bank for the buyer. Sellers who are not open to some form of seller financing will likely limit their possibilities of selling their business or need to discount the price to attract an all cash buyer, which are difficult to find. The majority of business sales include some form of seller financing.

Owner financing plays a key role in the overall structure of your business purchase. Essentially, depending on how much financing is available from asset based financing and how much existing liabilities we may assume, owner financing will fill the difference to finance the purchase price. We play around with these three figures, leaving the owner financing as a variable that we move up and down depending on the lending institutions and how much debt will stay with the business.

I like to build in a cushion on the owner financing side until we see how the lending institutions react from the financing of the assets and assumption of the liabilities. Once I get the responses back from the lending institutions and I have the amount of financing that we wanted, we can go back to the owner and reduce the owner financing. It plays out as a win-win transaction.

So let's put it all together through an example. In the diagram below, we reached a Business purchase price of $1,669,398 based on a 4X multiple of $414,850 of EBITDA. We will lower the cash need to pay for this purchase price by assuming the $693,12 in existing debt. This leaves us with $962,277 of the price we still need to pay for. Add to this $130,000 for other working cash needs and paying off closing fees to our lawyers and accountants. We now have to finance $1,096,277. We will finance $754,466 of this from Existing Cash, Accounts Receivables, Inventory and Equipment in the %s below. Leaving us with a financing need of $341,811. We will finance this with owner financing of $342,062, or 35% of the overall funds needed. ***This structure provides us with the ability to finance 100% of the purchase price.***

			Ebit	Multiple
Prcie of Business	1,659,398		414,850	4
Debt to be Assumed	**693,121**			
Price of Equity of Business		966,277		
Cash Needs				
Working Capital	**100,000**			
Fees	**30,000**			
Cash Out	**0**			
Total Cash Needs	**130,000**			
Purchase Price + Cash Needs		1,096,277		
Sources of Funding				
Assets For New Funding			**%**	
Cash	**70,149**	**70,149**	**100%**	
Accounts Recivables	**278,235**	**208,676**	**75%**	
Inventories	**487,523**	**195,009**	**40%**	
Equipment	**701,579**	**280,632**	**40%**	
Property	**0**	**0**	**00%**	
Total New Asset Funding		754,466		
Additonal Funding Needed		341,811		
Owner Financing		342,062	35%	
Other Funding Sources		(251)		

Lastly, we have to make sure that the business can pay for this additional financing. Assuming an average term of 10 years and an 8% annual interest rate for the new asset based lending, we would have to pay an additional $112,438 in debt per year. On the owner financing side, assuming a 5-year loan at 6% interest rate, we would have to pay an additional $81,145 in debt to pay the owner. With an EBIT of $414,850, we would still have $221,267 of EBIT left after servicing all the new debt for the owner's discretion. So this would be a fantastic deal with 100% financing.

EBITDA Projected		414,850	**Rate**	**Term (Yrs)**
New Debt Amortization		**($112,438)**	**8%**	**10**
Owner Financing		**($81,145)**	**6%**	**5**
Profit after New Debt Service		221,267		
New Debt Coverage Ratio		1.87		

Letter of Intent (LOI)

Once we have structured the deal, the financing we are going to require, the price of the business, and any specific terms we want to include, we are ready to send the seller a formal offer in the form of a Letter of Intent (LOI). The financing structure, the price, payment method, closing timing, and basic conditions to the sale will be included. The letter of intent may or may not be binding. As a rule of thumb, we want to make sure that it is non-binding with the exception of four things: exclusivity, ability to perform a due diligence, a precise time frame to close the purchase and a confidential agreement.

Confidentiality clauses are included in a business purchase letter of intent to describe how information shared between the parties should be protected and what information cannot be shared without the other party's consent. The confidentiality clause is, in effect, a non-disclosure agreement.

Things that need to be defined and included in the letter of intent are:

- Is it an Asset or Equity Purchase?
- The Purchase price
- What is the financing structure?
- What, if any, will the owner financing terms be?
- Access to the assets that are being used as collateral for the purchase such as equipment, inventory, real estate, and the accounts receivables
- Any conditions necessary regarding the lease such as landlord approval
- Any terms regarding key employees
- Closing subject to obtaining financing
- Any terms regarding the Seller's participation post-closing

- No material adverse changes to the business before closing

You want to reserve the right to change the purchase price subject to the due diligence with proper substantiation. If anything were to come up in due diligence that is material and that affects the earnings of the company or that adds an additional element of risk, and you're still willing to go forward with the deal, then you want to adjust the purchase price or the terms as a result of these findings. This can be achieved by an amendment to the letter of intent. In most cases, this may not be a factor but you want to reserve that right and option to change any terms of the LOI subject to the due diligence.

Be prepared for a negotiation. If none of these terms have been addressed or communicated during any of the meetings or subsequent communications between you and the Seller, this will be the first time that the Seller is seeing the price, financing structure, among other parts and he may be confused. I highly suggest you walk over every detail of the LOI with specific emphasis on the financing structure and price valuation with the Seller so that he understands your overall objective. There will probably be a number of rounds of negotiations. You may receive a counter offer that may affect the price, the structure, the owner financing or a combination of any one of these. You need to determine beforehand what the most important aspects of the deal are so you can negotiate accordingly. For example, if a 100% financed deal is the most important variable, to achieve this you may have to yield on price. You have to establish your thresholds and when the deal is no longer appealing. You have to have clarity on your "deal breakers" or walking away points. If the LOI is rejected outright, try to find out what exactly turned the seller off. Was it the price, the structure, the owner financing, the transition, the role he will play after wards?

Whatever it was, try to address it and weigh it against your deal breakers. Most deals that may appear to be "dead" can be salvaged. This takes patience and a keen ability to understand each other's walking away points. Try to determine the Seller's walking away points. And always stay true to yours. If there is no common ground, then the deal is not for you and move on.

Once both you and the Seller have agreed to a final Letter of Intent, it acts as a blueprint for drafting the final legal documents and helps both parties to reach an agreement on the material terms early in the process, and helps ensure any remaining issues get "out on the table" so they can be resolved early.

Chapter 12
Raising Capital

Raising capital is an intensive process and it's a skill set that you have to hone. Whomever has the ability to raise capital, who has that skill set, has a real competitive advantage. It's no different than sales. Anyone that can dominate the skillset of selling is going to have a competitive advantage. They are able to convince people. Whether it's selling something professional, selling an idea, negotiating with your personal relations, negotiating with your friends or even negotiating with your wife and children. The art of selling is no different than the art of fund-raising. The art of fund raising takes on an extra element of networking. Fund raising is a constant ability, yes to sell, but also to network. You never know where the funding is going to come from within your current or future network. So you have to evolve into a professional networker, you have to be a professional salesman.

I do not mean sales in the traditional sense; far from the image of a used car salesman. It's really more about the art of convincing. It's having the ability to state a case that is very hard to ignore. As the famous Marlon Brando said in The Godfather; *it's making an offer that you cannot refuse*. That's the art of professional sales and it is the essence of fundraising. It's the ability to convince. You have to have an audience to sell to. That is where the importance of your networking comes in. This is every day work. Every day you should be increasing your network for capital. Every day you should be reaching out and dealing with new people that could sometime in the future become a potential financier.

Let's talk about your appearance. How you present yourself is important. You have to present yourself as someone serious, someone people can trust. We mentioned the importance of improving and positioning yourself as a serious professional in social media profiles. First impressions, this is where that comes into play. People are going to do their due diligence on you and they're going to see if you are a serious person or somebody they can entrust their money to. It's very important how you present yourself on all platforms, especially in today's digital world. This does not mean you cannot have fun. Just do it in a tasteful manner. If you're doing things in a non-tasteful manner, well, keep those confidential and off the permanence of the internet. Keep your private life confidential not just for the sake of raising funds but also for the sake of your reputation in general. I cannot stress enough how many people get rejected, don't get a meeting or are cancelled on because of their social media presence.

Second, if this is your first deal, come to terms that you may not necessarily obtain 100% financing and you may need to bring in an equity player. That will entail possibly not owning 100% of the business. And that's OK. You may need to give up equity and raise capital into your deal so that you can have a deal. Why? Because you're not seasoned. You haven't done many deals like I have or other business acquirers have. You have to build up that rapport and that doesn't come overnight. It takes time. Be willing to leave or give other people equity more so than you probably would like. It's important for you to get the deal done. More deals will come after this one when you will have more prowess.

Third, you have to own the deal. It doesn't matter if you don't know much about finances, lending or equity. By all accounts, know your deal inside out! Be an expert in your deal. Know the benefits, the risks, the structure. You are selling this product. They're going to look to you to see if you know what you're talking about. So have a really good understanding of the business. You have to really understand the structure, and you have to really understand the risks and opportunities and be able to eloquently communicate all this. Do not think the deal itself will convince anyone. You have to know every aspect of your deal. The history, the owner, the product, the market, the financial structure, the opportunities, the risks, and ultimately the merits. They are going to be buying into you as much as the deal. The deal and you are one in the same to investors and lenders.

And lastly and probably most importantly, you have to truly believe it. Half the battle of convincing people is that they see how convinced you are. This becomes contagious. You're convincing them through communication, not necessarily through the deal. They need to see you so vested and so convinced of the merits of the deal that they want a part of it. You have got to position yourself as inviting them to an opportunity and less about asking them for money. There is a marked difference between *I have an opportunity for you that you cannot let slip away* and *can I borrow money for this venture*. You're inviting them to an opportunity that can make them money. That's very different than “I need money to finance a business purchase”. It is two very different proposition. People are now enticed. People want to be involved. People want to be business owners. You are essentially in a position to give them this. You need to play off this psychology. You are giving them an opportunity that they would otherwise not have. It is very powerful how this rubs off and how contagious this can be. The fact that you truly believe in it, that you know the deal inside out and that you're offering it as an opportunity, can make it irresistible. It makes it hard for people to miss out on. And it positions yourself for future deals should this opportunity be passed on by some.

This is the mindset that you need to absolutely have in capital raising. This is what you need to do to prepare yourself for financing. They will all look to you to preserve and "take care off" their capital. And they are comparing you to many other deals they have on the table. This is not much different than when you are positioning yourself with the owner. You have convinced the owner, and now you have to do the same and convince the financiers. Your mindset and ability to convince them by owning the deal and positioning it as an opportunity they cannot refuse is paramount to successful capital raising.

Lending Institutions

We have already talked about the various asset based lending sources in a previous chapter. We summarized real estate, accounts receivables, inventory and equipment financing. They all come, for the most part, from lending institutions. Lending institutions are the source that have the highest probability of a no personal cash down deal. The majority are going to be specialized asset based lending institutions. There's hundreds of institutions that specialize in equipment financing, commercial real estate financing, receivables financing, inventory financing and merchant cash advances. One only need to perform a Google search and will get numerous search results of prospective asset based financiers. I work with some very specific ones that I have established relationships with over the years. I'm always looking for new lenders because I want my financing to be as competitive as possible. There's always new lenders coming into the market offering new or different programs. These financiers are specialists in any particular asset class, and they do this day in and day out. This is what they focus on. They have seen every possible deal imaginable. They financed all types of businesses across all industries and sizes.

Don't think your deal is different or unique. Don't feel nervous or anxious about presenting your deal. They've seen it before and they deal with business buyers like you all the time. Many prospective buyers get stuck psychologically as if their deal was odd since this may be the first time they see a structure like this. You and your deal are not odd, but are one of many. They have business owners going to them, they have entrepreneurs going to them, they have people buying business going to them, they have existing clients going to them. This is their job. It's what they do and how they make a living. They are experts in this field and the asset class they specialize in. Introduce yourself. Talk about your deal. They're going to ask to see the specifics of it and they will analyze it like they do any deal. This encompasses all asset based lenders, including commercial banks. They will take the value of the asset and lend a percentage of its value. Below is the general rule of thumb on the maximum LTV per each asset class assuming existing assets and not new assets.

Asset Class	Loan to Value (LTV)
Receivables	90%
Inventory	50%
Equipment	50%
Real Estate	80%
Merchant Cash Advance	2.5 X Monthly Revenue

When you go to commercial banks, I would recommend going to local and regional banks as opposed to national and international banks. This is because the credit committees and the loan officers, the underwriters, are local and possibly physically at that bank. These banks tend to have a vested interest in the community. And the treatment is more personal. At the larger banks, the loan officers and they're underwriting departments are in different parts of the country or different parts of the world. They are dispersed. The person who will analyze and ultimately decide if your deal is approved is not going to be the person that you'll meet. Underwriting by definition is where all the documentation is submitted to, where the deal is analyzed and where a decision is made either by an individual or through a committee. The underwriting of your deal will be done somewhere else then the place where you originally submitted your loan request. The person that greeted you and attended you locally is your account manager. They have no decision making responsibilities. They are there more for informational purposes and to sell you the bank's products and services. However, if you go to a local or regional bank, you're probably going to meet the actual underwriters, the decision makers. You can establish a rapport and a relationship going forward. Now if you already have a relationship in place with a national one, then by all means, leverage that relationship. Also, most commercial banks, whether local or national, are SBA (Small Business Administration) qualified lenders. An SBA loan is a government-backed loan. The SBA (Small Business Administration) works with lenders to provide a partial guarantee of the outstanding loan balance to reduce the lender's risk and increases small business lending which helps to expand small business economic activity and are perfect for small business purchases. They don't finance 100% of a business purchase so you will need other sources of financing to complement them.

Owner/Seller Financing

Most small business sales are financed by the sellers themselves. Sellers of small businesses usually allow the buyer to pay some of the purchase price of the business in the form of a promissory note. This is what is known as owner or seller financing. This is another important part of our objective in not putting money down in the purchase of a business. In fact, it's estimated that over 50% of transactions include some form of financing from the former owner. While the percentages vary, the amount of seller financing is generally between 20% to 50% of the total purchase price, and I have seen some as high as 80%.

When you think about the situation, it makes perfect sense for the seller. First of all, by providing financing, the seller validates the viability of the business itself thereby attracting more buyers. Also, the seller is able to get the highest price possible by funding part of the acquisition. From a buyer's perspective, seller financing serves to reinforce that the business is sound because the seller is now at risk in the transaction. It's an insurance mechanism to help ensure that what you've been told by the seller is true and accurate. It serves as a mechanism to deal with situations that may arise later on that come about as a result of their actions where you may need the ability to offset. And equally important, you have the ability to get far more creative with seller financing. Seller financing can offer you better terms and a friendlier lender. You will be able to buy the business quicker because you won't have to wait a month for the bank's loan committee to meet. There is no loan processing or guarantee fees and, usually, no invasive lender controls or audits. While the terms vary for seller financing, you can expect to pay about 6-8% over three to seven years on average.

Leverage your Personal Assets

A lot of prospective buyers forget to look at their personal assets as a source of financing. They may not have much liquidity in their bank, but they may have assets. And if we want to achieve a no money down deal, always look at yourself and your assets as a source. This is the lowest hanging fruit for financing. The first and probably the most obvious asset is your home. You can refinance it and take cash out at closing for a down payment on a business purchase. Or you can get a home line of credit. This can be accomplished fairly fast, it is available, and it is cash that is stuck in an asset that is not producing any return. You will receive a better interest rate because the real estate backs up the loan. That would be the number one source when you're looking at getting debt financing from your personal assets. Remember, the existing cash flow from the business you are buying will repay this loan.

Another source is the use of credit cards. Apply for credit cards. I have over $250,000 worth of credit across 4 different credit cards. Now, I have been doing this for a long time so my credit is established. But you may have also build up your credit as well and you can have multiple credit lines available to you. I have seen people get approved for 10, 15, even 20 thousand dollars. If you apply to multiple credit cards, your credit capacity increases accordingly. While this is a more expensive, it is a source of financing to buy a business. The cash flow of the business will repay this debt. Don't think about credit cards as a long term solution, though. Think about them more like the merchant cash advance or a short term bridge loan to achieve your acquisition objective. It's a short term financing mechanism for you to finance part of the business acquisition

Other assets you may consider are Automobiles, Art, or Jewelry. If you do have a 401 k or an IRA account, this is also an asset where you can get financing for business acquisition. We are not implying to liquidate these assets or your 401(k). They all serve as collateral for a loan that can finance the purchase of a business. We usually don't think of using our wealth, our personal assets as means other than for our day to day living, to purchase and consume things. You are not using your capital and the source of repayment is the business. The business is going to pay that loan and the personal asset is still there. It is not much different than if you went out and got an asset based loan or a merchant cash advance. The business is going to pay that debt. Do not ignore the fact that you have financing capabilities right at your fingertips by leveraging your credit or most of your personal assets.

Friends and Family

Another source of financing are friends and family. These are people that know you. These are people that have a strong relationship with you. These are the people that naturally want to help. Now a lot of us have this mental block that we should never ask money from our friends and family. The question I pose to you is, why not? If it's a good opportunity, one that you think is going to make you money, why would you not offer that opportunity to your friends and family? You have done weeks if not months of research to find your ideal business and you are willing to change your life and your future because you believe in this opportunity. Why would you not offer the same opportunity to the people closest to you? This makes no sense. In other words, you're depriving them of an opportunity that you would take. Let me put it another way. If a vacation package came along at a deep discount, would you not share that with your friends and family? If you heard of a sale going on at a department store or a car dealership that was a great opportunity, would you not share that with your friends and family? I am not trying to be simplistic here or insult anyone's intelligence. You may be asking yourself, what does this have to do with buying a business? Well, when you share those things, your friends and family are going to be making a decision whether they want to buy the vacation or take advantage of the opportunity to buy a car or clothing or a TV or whatever the opportunity may be. They are mature enough to do so. They have enough information or will be resourceful enough to find it to make that decision. All you're doing is presenting them with an opportunity. They're equally mature enough and skilled enough to make a decision to either lend you money to buy a business or put equity into it. They, like the other opportunities, will see it as an opportunity or not. Do not make the assumption and make a decision for them. This is a mindset change you need to make.

If you truly believe in a business and you truly believe that you are the person that can make money from that business and create wealth, then, that's the how it should be presented to your friends and family. As the same opportunity you see. They can always say no. Rejection is part of raising capital. I have bought many businesses and I have had friends and family come to me and ask me why I didn't invite them and why I did invite a stranger or an institution. They have the right to ask me that. Why did I not give them that opportunity? And the truth is I do not have a good answer. Now I always invite them should the deal demand it. I make sure to tell my friends and family what I am doing, what the opportunity is all about and always leave it on the table for them to partake in it or not. I'm going to continue forward either way. But I always make it a point to involve my friends and family. Do not feel uncomfortable about it. Take that out of your mindset. Feel very comfortable because you are presenting them with an opportunity. It's up to them to decide whether that opportunity is good or not for them.

Extended Network

Another source of capital is your extended network, beyond your friends and family. This is no different than the points we made with regards to your friends and family. Offer them the opportunity that you see and have them make a decision. Now, whether for this deal or future ones, you should always be increasing your network. This applies not only for your current deal but think about the next deal. Right now, you're going to go out and contact your network to go raise capital. But tomorrow, you may have another deal or this deal may fall through.

You need to continuously knock on doors and build a network. Never stop knocking on doors. This may be uncomfortable but it is necessary. Rejection is normal and it's expected. Rejection will not only come from your network, it's going to come from the lending institutions, your friends and family. Rejection is just a part of raising capital. Accept it and move forward. Knock on as many doors. Just like deal sourcing, raising capital is a numbers game. Eventually, you're going to obtain the capital. But if you don't knock on enough doors within your immediate network and extended network, then the numbers are not going to be in your favor. Always build your network.

Angel Investors

Part of building your network is going to angel investors. These are people that actively finance or take equity positions in companies. You have to be able to identify them. If you go to the social media platforms, specifically LinkedIn and Facebook, search for business financiers, angel investors and other keywords related to angel investing or equity investments, buying businesses, financing transactions, mergers and acquisitions and so on. Your search will render hundreds of profiles. Reach out to these people and present yourself and start a rapport with them. Eventually you'll make them a pitch. You don't do that on first contact, but you do on the second or the third. Build a rapport and then you pitch them a deal.

You can find them in the various social media groups. Introduce yourself in these groups and start building rapport with some members. And eventually you pitch these deals to these people that are actively looking for deals. You can never stop looking for angel investors. They're constantly being offered deals so they have a pipeline of deals that is very large. They are quick to say no if they don't see the value in it. You're going to have to hone your pitch and continuously make it better. There's the famous "elevator pitch" analog whereby you have 30 seconds in an elevator to tell someone how good whatever you want to sell to them is. When both of you get to the bottom floor, they are able to understand the opportunity and make a decision, hopefully an affirmative one. It's the same thing with angel investors. You have to make a succinct business case for your business acquisition and why it's beneficial to them. This is no different what you are doing with all the other sources of debt financiers or equity financiers, just in a very condensed, and fast delivery format.

There are many networking groups that are set up around specific interest, hobbies and/or efforts. *Meetup.com* is the best platform where these groups reside and it is a very well known in the United States. I believe it's international. Find these Meetup groups, join them and attend their networking events. Be present at these groups whether you have a deal or not. If you have a deal you should be there. But if you don't have a deal, build rapport, build your network. Eventually, when you do have a deal, that rapport, that relationship will come into play. It's going to be a warm relationship with the members of these groups and so pitching the deal is going to be easier.

Crowdfunding

Crowdfunding is a newer platform as a means to raise capital. It is internet based. Crowdfunding is usually for non for profits and for startups, but also funds existing businesses and acquisitions. Many people invest in deals through raising money via many people or crowds. A deal is explained on these platforms and the type of funding is explained and opened to investors in blocks. People like you and myself can choose to invest a thousand dollars, ten thousand dollars, a hundred thousand dollars depending on the deal. You could raise capital for your deal by crowdfunding. You could pitch your deal to multiple strangers, via crowdfunding. This is a new form of raising money. Startups are very active in the crowdfunding platforms. If people are willing to take risks on startups, then presenting an established deal with mitigated risks should be a no brainer for a lot of these crowdfunding investors. I personally have never used crowdfunding to raise money for my deals. However, I do know of entrepreneurs that have raised money via the crowdfunding space as a source.

Confidential Information Memorandum

A Confidential Information Memorandum (CIM) is one of the first things an investor will ask for when you begin your capital raising mission. An CIM lays the foundation for your capital raising and sheds light on the past, present and future plans for your business. The CIM needs to show the business you are buying in the best light while giving potential buyers a realistic view of what they're buying, warts and all.

Following is an outline of the main headings you will need at a minimum when preparing an information memorandum for your capital raising:

1. Letter to Investors

This letter gives a summary of where you've been and where you plan to go. Keep it short and punchy and no more than a page in length.

2. Executive Summary

This section is a short excerpt of all the proceeding sections. It is designed to give a snapshot of your business and why you want to raise capital. It saves prospective investors the time of reading through an entire document. You want to give enough info here to keep investors interested but it is not meant to be comprehensive by any means. Think of it as a teaser to the rest of the content in your document. It is a chance to cover milestones that the business has achieved to date. In this section you must include a summary of the investment opportunity.

3. Background, Overview & History

Here you want to talk about the history of the company. When it started. What industry does it compete in. What the industry looks like. What have been important milestones. This section is to familiarize the investors with the actual business and it gives them strong context and perspective for the prospective investment.

4. Business plan and growth strategy

Now you're getting into the nitty-gritty. You want to give specific detail on the following aspects of your business at the very least:

- Market dynamics
- Corporate structure
- Your business model
- Key success factors
- Sales, Marketing and Customers

5. SWOT

You have to outline the Strengths, Weaknesses, Opportunities and Threats and eloquently relay them to prospective investors. Make sure you take time to understand in depth these 4 areas that envelop the business you want to buy.

6. Risks

Risk comes in many different shapes and forms, some of which you have control over and some of which you have none. You know better than anyone what the major risks are facing your business. You must be ready to have a plan in action to

MITIGATE these risks or reduce them significantly. This will be asked by investors. And if there are some risks that are out of your hands and are inherent to the business or industry then state it as such

7. Management Team

This is a big one. It is a good chance to extol the value of your team. You want to give more detail on your board of directors or advisory board members if you have one, your "Dream Team". Having a good management team is a big point of leverage as it shows reduced reliance on one key person with the backing, hopefully, of key executives via your board of directors or advisory board.

8. The Investment Offer

This is where you go into detail with regard to your investment offering. What will investors receive in return for investment in your business? If you're generating healthy profits and cash flow, then your focus will be on an appropriate earnings multiple combined with an assessment of strategic value to find a valuation. Here you are also going to present Return on Investment (ROI) and Payback scenarios for the investors so they know what the expected rate of return is for the investment and in what time frame.

9. Financial Statements and Forecasts

Most investors will want to see at least 3 years of operating history including Balance Sheet Income Statements. Then you want to also forecast these with the expected Sales increase and margin optimizations you plan to implement once you are the owner. These must be spelled out as assumptions so that investors can follow the forecasts.

10. How to Invest

Time to see the light and tell your prospective investors how they can apply for participation. If you need $500,000 are you raising these in lots of $50,000 or lots of $100,000 or just one lot for the whole amount.

This document is critical and will be asked for by angel investors, institutions and distant acquaintances. This document, while it is geared for equity investors primarily, should be given to all prospective financing sources. It doesn't matter whether it's your friends, your family, your immediate network or your extended network or some stranger you have just met. All of them are potential financiers, all of them are potential partners, all of them can lend you and or put in equity into the venture. All of them should be treated equally. I stress this because you have close relationships with some of these sources like your friends or your family. It does not mean that they should not receive the same amount of professionalism and seriousness as someone that you don't have a close relationship with. Do not confuse a friendship with a lack of formally. You are positioning yourself as a serious businessman with a serious deal. Your friends and family should receive the same degree of professionalism as angel investors and institutions. I stress this because I have seen it all too often that one takes informality and trust as a misguided sign that they have earned their friends or family's money. And that is not so. That needs to be earned no differently.

Chapter 13
Due Diligence

Due diligence refers to the process of evaluating a prospective business before purchasing. This will allow you the opportunity to thoroughly investigate all aspects of a business including the business's operations, financial performance, legal compliance, employee staff arrangements, customer contracts, intellectual property, assets and other details. This is your opportunity to assess the value of a business and the risks associated with buying it. There is often a lot more involved in operating a business that one might expect. If you don't do your due diligence you may end up making a bad decision and buy something that isn't as you thought, it would be. In particular, you should check that any information presented by the Seller (especially with regards to financial forecasts and reports) is accurate. You must satisfy yourself that the company is profitable and any projections as to future earnings are realistic and achievable.

When I started off doing this, I did the due diligence myself. Now I involve my accountant and lawyers to help with the due diligence for efficiency sake. However, you do not need to include any accountants or lawyers at this stage, it's really a question of comfort. If money is an object, then this is certainly something you can do yourself. You are verifying and validating a lot of the information you already know about the business. But what you definitely want to do is reach out to your lawyers and inform them that you are in the due diligence stage and that they should start getting ready or at least, to put it on your radar that, immediately after the due diligence, you're going to jump into the legal documentation of the business. I do involve my lawyers and accountants at this stage because I don't have time to go over every deal and every financial statement and every tax return. I do look at them but I don't do the actual due diligence alone.

Financial Due Diligence

In the financial due diligence, you're going to validate the income statements for the past three years as well as the balance sheet. You're going to want to look at their bank statements for this same time period. You need to understand the aging of their accounts receivables, any software reports coming out of whatever point of sale system they have or invoicing system. You going to analyze customer concentration in detail. You want to assure that their revenue is correct. That the expenses are correct. And the net income is correct. And you do this by reconciling the various financial reports with their bank statements. Their banks statements will ultimately capture all cash flow. Everything should go in and out of the bank statements; revenue and expenses, taxes and debt payments, interest and principal. And so you can certainly look at their financial statements and reconcile this with their bank statements. Look at cash inflows and cash outflows. Everything that is stated in the financial statements, the ones you used to value the business and structure the financing around, should reconcile with the bank statements. Any software reports coming out of their point of sale system or their invoicing system is where you can validate daily, weekly and monthly sales. The financial statements and bank statements should also be reconciled with the tax returns. Now mind you, there is tax treatment here and tax concepts that may be more complex to understand or reconcile. This is where the accountant comes in handy. You should analyze all the expenses that are listed in the various schedules of the tax returns, and match or correlate them to the bank statement, the income statement, and the balance sheet.

You are making sure that the earnings that were presented to you are there, that they exist. This is where the return on your investment will come from. This is what will be servicing the debt. So you want to be very comfortable with the results. If you're entertaining owners benefit or discretionary cash flow, this is exactly when you validate whatever add backs the owner has put in that owner's benefit or discretionary cash flow statement and make sure that they are valid add backs. I go in this with high skepticism. They need to prove to me that those add backs are actual business expenses and not personal expenses. If there's any deviations, you want to make sure that you get solid answers from the owner.

Also, you want to look at the asset side and liability side of the balance sheet. You should obtain a detailed list all of all the assets of the company. You want to pay close attention to cash on hand and average daily weekly and monthly balances. You want to look at the accounts receivables and specifically the aging of the accounts receivables. How many are current and how many are delinquent and for how long. The more pasts due the lesser quality they are. And some are uncollectible which will need to be written off. You will analyze the inventory. The owner should provide a list off all inventory. The important part about inventory is the state it is in. And when it was purchased. Has it been recently bought or has certain inventory been sitting in the warehouse for 6 months. Also, the inventory system being used is very relevant. You will do the same with fixed assets. You will want to count and evaluate the physical status of any machinery, equipment and tools. You will want to look at maintenance records and warranty service contracts. You do not want to buy a business and later realize you need to service the whole fleet and replace many parts because this has not been done in a while. The lending institution will validate these assets but will probably rely on you to do the heavy lifting and communications with the seller.

On the liability side, you will do the same, analyze current liabilities and long term liabilities, primarily loans and debt. You want to pay close attention to accounts payables, employee liabilities and taxes due. This is what needs to be paid in the short term. You may be assuming some or all of this as part of the purchase of the business. On the long term liabilities end, you are validating any existing debts. You will want to confirm maturities, term, interest rate and any significant covenants. Remember, you are analyzing more from a financial stand point and assuring that what you see is consistent with the financial picture given by the various financial statements. It sounds more complex than it really is.

Legal Due Diligence

Understanding the corporate books is vital when we're buying the company as an equity transaction. If it as an asset purchase, then they are not relevant. You need to have access to all the corporate books. You want to understand the articles of incorporation, all board meetings and shareholder/member meetings and what decisions were approved. You want to understand the operating agreement of the entity you're buying. You also want to make sure all the legal documents and the corporate books are up to date. That said, I have run into all types of businesses. I have run into businesses that are owned by one person whose corporate books are excellent. And I have seen the opposite side of the spectrum where there are no corporate books other than the articles of incorporation, the tax I.D. number, and the blank shares. Some owners have never held a meeting. This is common. The owner is a sole owner and has never needed to keep the corporate books intact. This does have an easy solution. Before he sells, he can have a meeting whereby he approves everything that he's done in the past and gives you the corporate books intact. Your lawyer should make sure that all this occurs during the legal documentation phase. You want to make sure the entity is in good standing. In the United States, you check with the secretary of state of where the company is operating and at the federal level that the company is in compliance with all filing requirements.

You want to make sure that there's no past or present lawsuits or anything having to do with litigation, whether with suppliers, clients, employees or partners. This is the time where you want to make sure you understand any litigation risks as this could be a deal breaker depending on the nature of the lawsuit and the potential damages. Remember, in an Equity purchase you are inheriting the history of the entity. So any actual or contingent legal matters should be understood thoroughly. You want to analyze and verify any permits, licenses or certifications that you would need to run the business.

You want to review all contracts with the clients, the suppliers, and the employees. This is a good time to see what legal obligations the company has with all these actors. You want to check the lease agreement. You need to understand if the landlord needs to approve any significant change in ownership. If it's an Asset purchase, you want to be able to assume the existing lease or renegotiate a new one. You want to validate if there's additional options to renew. There's been cases where I bought a business and they had six months left in the lease. I needed to know this at this stage because if not, the landlord could essentially kick us out six months after I had purchased. Also, you want to familiarize yourself with terms and conditions of the leases as well as any restrictions

Commercial Due Diligence

From the commercial standpoint, this encompasses both customers and suppliers. The customer base is another important area and the key customer contracts need to be analyzed carefully. Are the contracts clear, fair and are they going to be affected by a change of ownership? What are the terms and conditions and are there any significant customer issues? What shape is the sales pipeline and the sales team in?

Other main questions you might want answered are:

- How long have they been customers?
- Who is their main contact at the business? If this is the owner, how will his / her departure affect the relationship and should you consider his /her continued involvement for a period of time?
- What is good and bad about the business' products or services?
- Who are your competitors and do your customers also use them? If so, why, and how do you compare / compete?

- What will the customers' future demand be for the business' products or services?

Almost as important as your customer base, are your suppliers and distribution channels. These can reveal a great deal about the target company. In particular, you need to know:

- Are the supplier contracts clear, fair and are they going to be affected by a change of ownership?
- What are the terms and conditions and are there any supplier issues? Are there any areas that are vulnerable and are there any issues or potential issues in respect of either suppliers or distribution? Are your suppliers' practices ethical?
- Does the business pay on time and is the target company an efficiently run business which treats its suppliers well?

Employee Due Diligence

At the heart of any good business are the management team and employees. Due diligence should at least include:

- Full details of management profiles and organization.
- Details of all employee profiles including salary, benefits, incentives and perks and any misconduct or professional development issues.
- Contracts of employment. Has the target company got measures in place to prevent key members of staff leaving or being stolen? How is employee morale and what is staff retention like?

- Copies of any pension, profit sharing, deferred compensation, and retirement plans. It may be necessary to take actuarial advice on the valuation of a pension fund.
- Employment manuals and policies.

You also want to look at the employee files. You want to see what type of applications have been filled out, what forms have been signed, whether they signed a non-compete agreement protecting any secrets or protecting the company's way of doing business. You want to see if they consented to random drug tests, if there's any criminal records, if there's any complaints or any reviews, if there's been any salary raises or hourly raises. Look for any evidence of disgruntled employees. You want to analyze scheduling and overtime. Make a mental note of how you could create efficiencies by reducing overtime. In the United States, one pays one and a half times the hourly wage should they go past 40 hours a week. So overtime costs can be excessive. I've bought many companies that have excessive over times and putting the right processes in place, the right shifts in place, reducing if not eliminating overtime is a very simple thing to do. And this benefit goes right down to the bottom line as profit.

Fixed Assets Due Diligence

In analyzing fixed assets look at all the equipment. You need to account for all of these assets. Understand the condition. Understand the maintenance history, what logs are being kept for maintenance, parts and repairs. Understand if you're going to have a need to start replacing the equipment in the near future. There are instances when people acquire really poor equipment because the seller has just been putting off much needed maintenance. You might want to adjust the purchase price based on what those estimates would be to repair should anything be significant. You want to verify any warranty or service contracts in place. Determine if there is a malfunction, is it covered under an existing warranty or will it cost money to repair. Start making mental notes when analyzing the assets as to what you may need as you grow the business. This is not necessarily a due diligence issue. But if you want to scale the business, what kind of capital expenditures will you need to make in the future? What does this entail in terms of capital needs, delivery times, among other things?

During the due diligence period, if any serious issues are uncovered, it may be appropriate for you to renegotiate the deal or even to cancel it. You need to be comfortable with all aspects of a business and understand all of the risks involved before purchasing. I recommend that you invest time and resources into the due diligence process before buying a business. This will minimize the possibility of anything unexpected occurring/coming to light after the business is bought. A quality due diligence investigation carried out is vital in buying a viable and successful business. By no means this is not a comprehensive due diligence list. It really depends on the type of business you are buying, the size, the industry, among many other variables. All these areas stated above are common areas that should be included in all due diligence efforts.

Chapter 14
Legal Documents and Closing

Once the due diligence stage ends and the parties are locked into the deal, then it is time to prepare the definitive acquisition documents and address all the logistics necessary for closing. Assuming that everything went well in the due diligence; whether there was a need to amend the letter of intent or not, the actual legal documentation process takes place. At this stage I highly recommend to contract a lawyer if you have not already done so. The heavy lifting going forward will be done between the lawyers of the buyer and the seller. Our lawyer will now be advising us and negotiating all the legal terms and documents with the seller's attorney. We need to make sure all the information we have up to this point is fully transmitted to our lawyer if we have not done so already. Our lawyer will prepare the purchase agreement and all the other legal documents such as employment agreements, address any environmental issues, and any permits certifications or licenses. If owner financing is involved, they will redact the promissory notes and the security agreement if applicable. If it's an equity purchase, they will address all the corporate documentation and make sure it is order and up to date. If it's an asset purchase, they will draft the bill of sale. They will coordinate with all the lending institutions and the necessary documents as well as help with escrow or disbursements of funds at closing. If there exist any extraordinary circumstances or agreements, this needs to be explained and communicated to the lawyers so that they can properly documented in the legal documents. And they will address in conjunction with the seller's lawyer any and all other pertinent legal documents and closing logistics.

Purchase Agreement

The most important legal document is the purchase agreement or the sales agreement. A Purchase/Sales Agreement is the legal document that specifies all of the terms and conditions associated with the purchase and sale of a company or the assets. The document outlines the price, the payment method, the representations and warranties, and any conditions. Once signed by the buyer and seller deal is considered closed. Now, it is important to understand that this phase of the transaction is really the last stage. After this stage you will have bought the business. However, negotiating the purchase agreement is equally as complex as negotiating the business itself. As previously mentioned, all the business criteria conditions; the purchase price, the structure, employee retention, the owner transition or involvement as a consultant or as an employee, owner financing and any other business aspect has already been agreed upon. The purchase agreement is where all this is spelled out the way we as the buyer and the seller have agreed. What the seller interprets and what you interpret and how this gets written into the legal documents may leave room for further negotiations. Even though, we're at the last phase of the business buying process, there's going to be back and forth so that the seller and the buyer can ultimately agree on the language. Should there be problems after the purchase, we're going to refer back to these documents, particularly the purchase agreement to seek any restitution or to come to some sort of agreement between the buyer and the seller.

Representations and Warranties

Probably the most important part of the purchase agreement are the representations and warranties and the associated indemnifications. You as a buyer have relied on all the information that the seller has given. Even if the buyer conducts a thorough due diligence, the buyer typically is at an informational disadvantage relative to the seller. This is because the buyer lacks the seller's level of knowledge of the target. No buyer can reasonably expect to verify every detail about the target business during due diligence.

A representation is a "statement made by one of two contracting parties to the other, before or at the time of making the contract, in regard to some fact, circumstance, or state of facts pertinent to the contract, which is influential in bringing about the agreement, as defined by Black's Law Dictionary online. Seller representations exist because it is virtually impossible for the buyer to verify every detail about the target. The seller's representations and warranties serve a three-fold purpose from the buyer's perspective:

1. To assist the buyer in understanding the business it is purchasing
2. To protect the buyer from not having full insight into the business that it is purchasing, by allowing the buyer to abort the transaction if it finds the representations misleading before the closing

3. To enable the buyer to recover damages if the seller's representations and warranties materially or fraudulently misrepresent the reality of the business

The buyer relies on the seller's representations and warranties as all-inclusive of the target company's financial and operational position. For example, the seller may represent that "neither the description of the business and properties of the corporation, nor the financial statements, contain any untrue statement of a material fact or omit to state any material fact necessary to make the statements or information therein not misleading."

Many of the topics typically covered by the seller's representations and warranties are:

- Corporate authority to execute the transaction agreement

- Organization, standing, and qualification of the target company

- Financial statements of the target company, including the following:

    - The nature of the financial statements

    - The target company's assets, such as real property, inventory, other tangible personal property, accounts receivable, trade names, trademarks, copyrights, patents and patent rights, trade secrets, and other intangible property

    - All debts, obligations, and liabilities of the target company

- Statements to ensure that target tangible and intangible assets and liabilities are what the buyer expects them to be, and that the buyer is acquiring the assets unencumbered (unless otherwise stated)

- Tax returns and audits of the target company
- Capital structure of the target company
- The solvency of the target company immediately after closing
- Identification of customers and the seller's interest in customers, suppliers, and competitors
- Warranty promises or contracts with clients
- Existing employment contracts
- Corporate documents and other contracts, agreements, and obligations
- Compliance with relevant authorities
- Existence of known or impending litigation
- Identification and compensation of officers and directors
- Statements regarding changes or the absence of changes to the financial position, operations, liabilities, assets, business, or prospects of the target company since the date of the last audited financial statements
- The statement of full disclosure

Each of these (and other) items can be further described in a supporting schedule or exhibit to the transaction agreement.

Representations can include the most contested aspects of a transaction, or they can include standard language that is present in virtually all transactions. The exact wording of the seller's representations is negotiated between the buyer's lawyer and the seller's lawyer. Naturally, the buyer prefers stringent language and broad warranties, and the seller prefers the opposite. If the representations are narrower than the buyer anticipated, additional due diligence may be required. If the representations specifically exempt certain issues, this may be a sign that there is a problem or that the seller does not have specific knowledge of those issues.

How much or how little the seller is willing to represent to the buyer can affect how much the buyer is willing to pay to acquire the target. If the buyer perceives that the seller's representations are narrow and include ambiguous language, then the buyer may perceive the investment to be riskier—and the buyer may demand a lower price to offset the additional risk. Of course, transactions are not negotiated, executed, and completed all on the same day. Therefore, seller's representations are specific to a particular point in time. Depending on the specific representation and the goals of the parties, representations can be accurate (1) as of the date of the financial statements, (2) at closing, (3) at signing, (4) for some period after the closing of the transaction, or (5) for some combination of items one through four.

Buyers typically require that a seller's representation be included in the purchase agreement. This is because if any part of the seller's representations turns out to be false, the seller may be liable for any economic damages incurred by the buyer. The buyer and seller can negotiate the seller's liability for misrepresenting facts in a number of ways, including the following:

- Holding back a portion of the purchase price for a specified period of time.
- The indemnification clause in the transaction agreement.

As a result, the representations and warranties section is probably the section that's the most sensitive and highly negotiated of the legal document phase. The buyer wants to be as protected as possible and the seller doesn't want future liability or exposure and thus wants to give as little representations and warranties as possible. It is not necessarily because the seller is trying to hide something, sometimes it is, but more so because he knows that should something go wrong in the future, the buyer can and will seek remedy and indemnification for anything that happened in the future that was represented to him and warrantied in this legal document. He may seek damages to the point of reverting the transaction. This is why this section is very sensitive and highly controversial. In fact, deals do fall apart due to the sensitivity of this section.

Purchase Agreement Revisited

Other key provisions or sections of a purchase agreement are:

A Description of the Parties: The purchase of a business or assets has a buyer and a seller and both parties are named in the agreement. The parties are the participants who sign the contract so you should make sure that the name or names in this section represent the people or entities that should be listed as the responsible parties for the contract.

A Description of the Item Being Sold and an Agreement to Sell: A purchase sale agreement will always identify what is being sold and what the financial terms of the agreement are. This section will indicate whether equity or assets is being sold and will state the purchase price. The method of payment must be specified and this will usually either be the financing structure agreed to including owner financing, lending institutions, cash or a combination of all. If debt is used, this section will usually refer to an Appendix that provides additional details related to the financing.

Covenants after Closing: If the closing is to occur after signing the purchase and sale agreement, the it is customary to include covenants to protect the business and operations and to limit the amount of new liabilities the company may take on. For example, these covenants usually require the seller to continue to operate the business in the regular fashion and to inform the buyer of any material changes.

Closing Conditions: Closing conditions are conditions which must occur before the parties are obligated under the terms of the Purchase and Sale Agreement. These are determined largely by what consents and approvals are needed and may include, for example: landlord approval.

Restrictive Covenants After the Closing: The Purchase and Sale Agreement also usually includes covenants that restrict the operations of the business. These are included in order to protect the business and operations of the company after closing. These fall into three basic categories: a) non-solicitation of customers; b) non-solicitation of employees; and c) competition. These provisions must be carefully drafted with an attorney to make sure that the provisions are enforceable.

Boiler Plate Language: Purchase and Sale Agreements will also all contain boiler-plate language that addresses a number of different legal aspects. Some of the boilerplate language includes:

- Which Governing law applies
- A statement indicating that the document represents the entire agreement between the parties
- A statement regarding headings and organization and their impact
- A statement that if one part of the agreement is deemed not valid, the rest of the agreement is valid
- A statement of how modifications to the document must occur (usually in writing)
- A statement regarding how notices, law suits and expenses should be handled

Bill of Sale

If it's an equity purchase, then the assets are owned by the legal entity so there's no need to define what assets are being purchased and what assets are being excluded. However, if it is an asset purchase, then we will need a bill of sale. The bill of sale is a document that lists every single asset that you will be buying. All the equipment, machinery, office supplies, inventory, furniture, fixtures, telecommunications system, technology equipment, among other assets. All the assets that are being purchased need to be detailed and priced as those assets will form part of the new balance sheet going forward and will also be your cost basis for tax reporting purposes. Any intangible assets such as trademarks, trade secrets, brands, logos, Web sites also form part of the bill of sale. Any assets that are excluded need to be determined and marked as excluded assets.

Non-Compete Agreement

Another document is the non-compete document. This document states that the seller will not be able to compete for a given length of time, in a given geographic radius. As an example, if we're buying an Italian restaurant, the seller may not start a new Italian restaurant within a 15-mile radius for the next 5 years. If it's a service company and you're servicing the Chicago metro area, the geographical radius may be 100-mile radius. Included in the non-compete agreement traditionally is a non-solicitation clause. This means that the seller may not solicit employees to go work for him or our clients to do business with him

The strategy we like to employ is not to use the traditional non-compete agreement. We use a compete agreement. So the seller may start a competing business immediately after closing. However, we place specific terms, for instance: if the seller does employs a current or past employee, they will have to pay us a fixed amount per employee i.e. $25,000 per employee. With regards to clients, if they sell to our client base, they will pay us 50% of the invoice price into perpetuity. What we're accomplishing is making it very difficult and costly for the seller to compete with us. There will be an immediate cost if he's going to take our employees or try to take our clients. Legally, it is very difficult to enforce a non-compete agreement. It is costly, you have the burden of proof, and it is very difficult to prove. If you bought an Italian restaurant and the Seller starts a Pizzeria restaurant with Italian dishes, is he really competing? In practice, lawyers have a difficult time enforcing the non-compete agreement. If we do a compete agreement, then it's easier to enforce. You simply invoice them for any clients of ours that they are servicing and invoice them for any employee of ours that they have hired. From a legal standpoint, it is easier to enforce, it is more strategic and becomes a great deterrent.

Transition Agreement

Another important and common document is the transition agreement. We like to make sure that the owner stays on for at least 90 days after the closing to train and assure a smooth transfer of ownership. Some sellers want to move on as soon as possible and will likely ask for not more than 30 days. Whatever the time frame, there will be a transition period. The owner stays on board without compensation to help in transitioning clients, employees, suppliers and any operational items that need to be addressed apart from general training on all operational aspects. It's generally considered part of the purchase price. If the seller is going to be employed or have a consulting agreement after the transition period, then that needs to be spelled out and form part of the transition agreement or may be a separate agreement altogether. The main difference is that during the transition period, the seller will not be receiving any compensation as that is already incorporated into the purchase price. After the transition period, if the former owner stays in some capacity, then compensation is expected.

Promissory Note and Security Agreement

Another document is the promissory note. The promissory note is necessary only if the seller has agreed to owner financing. The business will have a promissory note and a debt payable to the former owner. Most promissory notes have a 5 to 7-year time frame and command 6-8% interest rates. Accompanying the promissory note may be a security agreement. A security agreement may take certain business assets as collateral for the promissory note. In the event that the business fails to pay on the promissory note, then the owner now has recourse through this security agreement and can either take over the assets, if assets are securing the promissory note or can even take over a percentage of the shares of the company or a hundred percent of the shares of the company if the business fails to pay on the promissory note.

Checklist for Minimum Documents Required for Closing		
Equity purchase		Asset Purchase
Stock or LLC Memebership Certificates		Bill of Sale
Purcahse Agreement		Purcahse Agreement
Promissory Note		Promissory Note
Security Agreement		Security Agreement
Corporate or LLC Record Book		Consent of Entity Owners for Asset Sale
Resignation of Directors and Officers		Non-Compete Agreement
Non-Compete Agreement		Transition Agreement
Transition Agreement		Employment or Consulting Agreement Previous Owner
Employment or Consulting Agreement Previous Owner		Assignment of Lease
Landlord's Consent		Assignment of Intellectual Property
Contracts with Clients and Suppliers		Assignment of Client and Supplier Contracts

Chapter 15
Closing and Final Tips

The day of the closing is pretty uneventful. All the hard work, the heavy lifting, has been done in the previous phases. You have already done the due diligence. You've already raised funds from financiers. The lawyers have finished negotiating and have drafted up and negotiated all the legal documents that need to be included in the closing. They have also coordinated with the financiers and lending institutions for money and capital distributions. The financiers just need confirmation that that deal has been consummated. The money may be already sitting in an escrow account with your lawyer or with a title company coordinated by your lawyer. Everything has already been signed off by your lawyers and more importantly signed off by the buyer and the seller. All of this has already been accomplished. The day of the closing is signing the approved documents. The closing really is uneventful. I know you'll be very enthusiastic because you will now be the owner of a business. All this hard work is materializing into your business purchase. But the actual day is just signing all these to transfer ownership over. Again, this is not so different from buying a home as we have mentioned many times.

There is a lot of documents to be signed. Both you and the seller will need to initial must pages and sign where necessary. There will be a couple of copies of all the documents, one for yourself, one for the seller and one for each lawyer. Once all of the pages have been signed and collected, your lawyers or the title company will then inform the financiers, the lending institutions, the investors or whomever is helping you or partnering with you to buy the business that everything has been complete. They may need to fax proof of all this. Once accomplished, the wire transfers will be executed or the escrow money will be released. Legally you have become the owner of the company.

Congratulations, it is a big moment for you. Although an uneventful day, the fun part is really just about to start!!!

Tips for After Day of Closing

The first thing you want to do is have an employee meeting and you want the former owner to be there with you. At this meeting, you should explain to the employees that you are now the owner. You're going to want to reassure them that everything is going to be great, that the business has a bright future, that the owner is going to help out for 30, 60, or 90 days, whatever time frame you negotiated, training you as well as helping through the transition. If he's going to stay out as a consultant or as an employee, that needs to be said at this meeting and explained in detail what that entails exactly.

Secondly, it is important that you kindly but emphatically state that even though the owner will be present, whether it's short term or long term, you want it to be clear to both him and the employees how the transition will work. Remember the employees have for months, if not years been reporting to the owner. It's a natural habit that they're probably going seek the owner if he's physically there. So you want to be very clear that you are the “go to” person going forward. Even though the owner is going to be advising you, everything now needs to go through you. There needs to be a mindset shift of breaking the habit of going to the former owner with any questions or requests for approval or any specific guidance on decisions that need to be made. Really, there's no correct way of doing this or one specific way. Just be very mindful of the former owner and be clear. Say something like, *"I'm excited that Mr. Jones has decided to stay during this transition or more on a permanent basis. I will be taking over the day to day business operations and running it and he will be helping me and advising me through this so that we all can make the most of this swift transition."* Use your own words and your own style, but do draw a line in the ground in an amicable but definitive way.

Third, take control of the cash. Understand immediately how much cash is in the bank. What are the immediate cash needs? What's going to be paid in the next 4 weeks? What revenue is coming in? You should probably have a very good idea about this because of your due diligence, but you want to make sure that you control it. The number one reason why small businesses fall into trouble is because they run out of cash as a result of not understanding or controlling their working capital. It's not that the business is not doing well, there may be lags between cash coming in and cash going out. What you do not want to happen is there to be a deficit. You should have planned for this in your deal structuring as part of your working capital financing. It's going to be very different how the previous owner ran it and how you're going to run it in terms of cash and who approves what. Before you can even implement new systems and processes, you need to make sure that the cash on hand and the cash that's going to be spent and that's coming in is under your control. You should create a daily cash needs for the next 3 months. You should understand the daily uses and sources of funds for the next 90 days.

Fourth, make a plan to reach out to your clients. If possible, take the former owner with you or have them in a conference call with you so he can officially introduce you and reinforce what a great decision it was for him to hand over the reins to you. This is a great ice breaker and a natural point of transition. The clients will need it as much as you will. What you want is for the client to start talking to you. Him introducing you is that very bridge. Then you relay to them that you're going to be talking to them to fully comprehend the client relationship, understand their needs, and any contextual or idiosyncrasies that each client may have. This is important so that you can factor those in to your decision making and you could start getting to know your clients and your clients can start getting to know you.

Lastly, avoid the urge to start changing everything immediately. This is where a lot of people make very poor judgment decisions. They want to start changing everything at once. They do not have context, perspective or understand all the different moving pieces at this stage. Wait and learn, gain experience, gain perspective. If your plan entails cutting a lot of the wasteful spending, reducing the staff, cancelling poor performing clients, replacing suppliers, looking into different office configurations, whatever it is that you want to do, wait! Do not rush and certainly do not make any big decisions within the first few months. You have not fully grasped the day to day operations and the nature of this business. This takes time and you need to have that time to really understand the "A to Z" of this company. You "get it" from a 40,000-foot level but you have not been there day to day. Many things happen on a day to day basis in any one business for a reason. You need to understand before you start making any changes. What you do not want to do is start making changes in processes, in the way business is conducted with clients, in terms or pricing or switching supplier's terms, to then find out that the quality is wrong or your clients aren't paying on time or the morale of your employees is being affected. There is a "method to the madness" you need to grasp before you can distinguish the good from the bad.

And change is hard for everyone. Do not underestimate this. Your employees, clients and suppliers, in various degrees, are all going through an emotional rollercoaster ride with the transfer of ownership. They're excited but they're also apprehensive and may be scared because they don't know you. You do not want change to backfire on you. Specifically, with your employees, change is significantly harder. New owner implies changes and many will be nervous about their job security. This does not only apply to the big decisions, but small decisions as well. Do not go and rush to change the layout of an office space, or change the phone systems, or software system, or even the small benefits they receive in terms of coffee, water, sodas, breaks, etc. There's a why and a reason for the way things are and the employees are used to that. This is their Culture. Give it time. Get to know the employees, get to know the whys, ask a lot of questions, understand the culture. Win them over first.

Little by little start making decisions and see if these decisions are correct. Most will be correct but some will be wrong and you want to look at. You're also here guiding the employees, they're looking at you, they're seeing if this person is a leader. They're sizing you up so you want to minimize the mistakes, especially avoidable ones. You want to make sure you are giving the right impression, and the right message, and the right communication to your employees, to your clients, to your suppliers that you know what you're doing. With few exceptions, nothing material is going to happen in the first 30 to 60 days. You have just bought the business. You will have time to make any and all change that are necessary.

This is an exciting time. You're going to be very busy. There's a lot of information you have to assimilate, you have to take in. You've got to let it marinate. But, eventually, you're going to get it. Some business owners, new business owners get it faster than others. Now that you're a business owner you get to thrive.

So, Congratulations! It's an exciting time. You've accomplished that financial independence, you're your own boss, you have achieved professional independence, and now you are the captain of your own ship. You are now in a position of creating wealth.

Make the most of it!

About the Author

Arturo has been an entrepreneur, a sought after consultant/coach and public speaker for over 25 years. He has been involved in well over 130 business purchases, transactions, engagements and business deals.

He has successfully started, bought and or sold over 45 national and international companies, personally from his own portfolio, primarily in the small business space. In some cases, with operating partners. He has bought restaurants, started a tequila company, a consumer goods export company, a technology company, bars and night clubs, a pest control company, fast food restaurants, real estate brokerages, a steel fabrication company, franchises, a wholesale distributor, a Data Center, a loan servicing company, a logistics company, an import and distributor of electrical appliances, an oil and gas company, a theater production, a professional soccer game, a senior living management company, among others. These have all been done for his own portfolio and in many cases without using his own capital.

He has raised money from angel investors. He has raised millions of dollars from venture capital funds like Merrill Lynch Venture Capital, CVC Latin America, Citibank's venture capital arm as well as Explorador fund in Silicon Valley. He has taken a company public on the stock market in the United States. He has also been involved in corporate takeovers as an entrepreneur. He has raised millions of dollars from banks, asset based lending institutions and angel investors. All of this for his portfolio companies previously mentioned.

He has worked at Goldman Sachs, Bank of America, Lehman Brothers, and KPMG as managing director of their mergers and acquisitions division where he was involved in over 90 deals.

As a professor he has taught courses in *Investment Analysis, Corporate Finance and Capital Administration* at the graduate and undergraduate level.

He holds a Masters of Business Administration from the Kellogg Graduate School of Management at Northwestern University and a Double Masters in International Relations and Communications from Boston University.

To receive updates, special offers and future products please sign up at:

www.arturohenriquezauthor.com

Made in the USA
Monee, IL
04 September 2021